D1253353

WITHDRAWN

GUADALCANAL

BY THE AUTHOR

IRVING WERSTEIN

Guadalcanal

MAPS BY AVA MORGAN

THOMAS Y. CROWELL COMPANY

NEW YORK

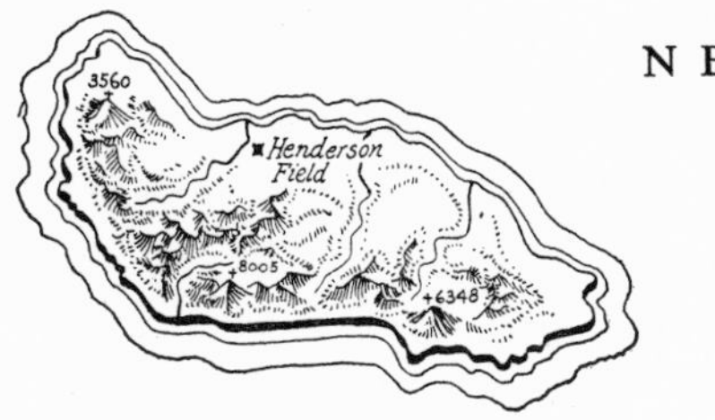

Manufactured in the United States of America by the Vail-Ballou Press, Inc., Binghamton, N.Y.

Library of Congress Catalog Card No. 63-15099

FIRST PRINTING

This book is for my friend

MME. MADELINE NICE,

an undaunted soul

"AND WHEN HE GOES TO HEAVEN

TO SAINT PETER HE WILL TELL:

ANOTHER MARINE REPORTING, SIR;

I'VE SERVED MY TIME IN HELL!"

Poem by an anonymous
Guadalcanal Marine
inscribed on the cross that
marked a comrade's grave.

AUTHOR'S NOTE

The Battle of Guadalcanal began in August, 1942, and lasted until February, 1943. It was a long, tedious struggle; a nightmare that went on for six months.

In this book, I have attempted to convey some of the pain, terror, and misery that young Americans faced on Guadalcanal. War is horrendous and was made even more so by the jungles, diseases, heat, and foulness of Guadalcanal.

No man who fought there will forget the ordeal he survived. In the Pacific War, all the island fighting was vicious and bitter. There were battles on Iwo Jima, Okinawa, Tarawa, Saipan, New Britain, and many places more but none equaled Guadalcanal if only because the others did not continue as long.

At Guadalcanal, the Japanese learned how Americans could fight. That battle, on a remote island thousands of miles from the shores of the United States, ranks in historical importance with Bunker Hill, Gettysburg, Château-Thierry and even D-Day, for Guadalcanal was also a turning point. It marked an end to unbroken Japanese successes in the Pacific and the start of the American march to victory.

It would have been impossible in a work such as this to present all the complexities of the Battle of Guadalcanal. I have condensed much of the six-month-long action in this effort to make it live for a generation of readers yet unborn in 1942.

I have stressed the part taken by the 1st Marine Division in the Guadalcanal campaign, fully aware that other Marine units, and U.S. Army divisions as well, also participated in the struggle.

My purpose was not to glorify any outfit. Nor did I intend to ignore any. The 1st Marine Division planted the American flag on Guadalcanal to open the initial U.S. offensive in the Pacific. Since the story of the battle is a saga of American courage and resoluteness, I have recounted it through the experiences of the 1st Marine Division. What those men endured happened to everyone who followed their footsteps into the dank and malodorous jungles of Guadalcanal against a wily and resourceful enemy.

I was aided by many people during the research and writing of this book. As usual, Dr. James J. Heslin and the staff of the New-York Historical Society were both patient and efficient. I received assistance from the Marine

Corps Historical Branch and the U.S. Army Office of the Chief of Military History, Washington, D.C.

But the most invaluable help came from men who had fought on Guadalcanal and were willing to talk about it. I especially wish to thank William Geyer for his vivid recollections of his days on Guadalcanal, that place the Japanese renamed Death Island. I also thank Mr. John J. Flanagan for his courtesy in arranging my meeting with William Geyer.

J. J. Tarrant, Lt. USNR (Ret.), clarified for me the intricacies of naval warfare so this landlubber could understand the sea fighting that raged in the waters around Guadalcanal.

Learning the truth about what happened at Guadalcanal was greatly simplified by Samuel Eliot Morison's *The Struggle for Guadalcanal.* I owe him a tremendous debt of gratitude.

My wife and young son steered clear during working hours and my agent, Miss Candida Donadio, was always ready with a word of encouragement when the going got rough.

I. W.

NEW YORK, N.Y.
MARCH, 1963

CONTENTS

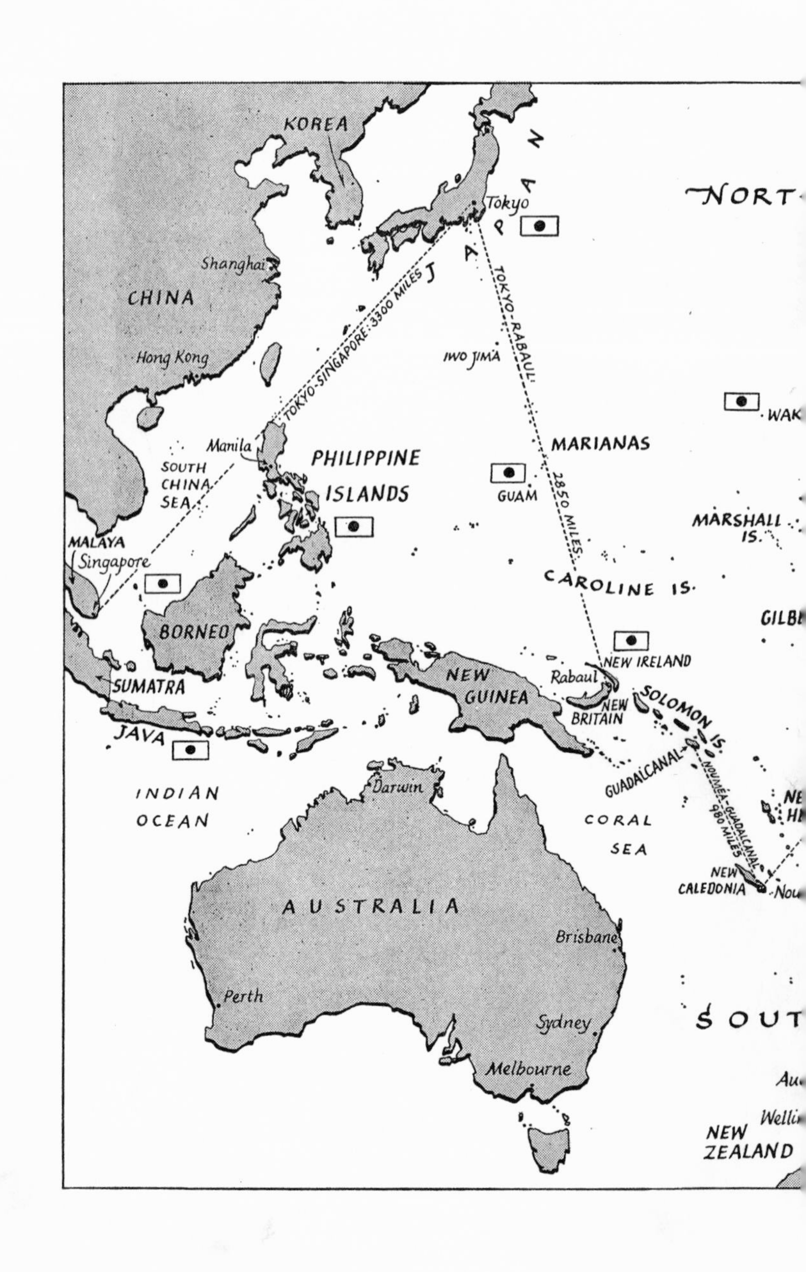
KOREA
JAPAN
Tokyo
NORT
Shanghai
CHINA
TOKYO-SINGAPORE 3300 MILES
TOKYO-RABAUL
Hong Kong
IWO JIMA
WAK
Manila
PHILIPPINE ISLANDS
MARIANAS
SOUTH CHINA SEA
GUAM
2850 MILES
MARSHALL IS.
MALAYA
Singapore
CAROLINE IS.
GILB
BORNEO
NEW IRELAND
Rabaul
SUMATRA
NEW GUINEA
NEW BRITAIN
SOLOMON IS.
JAVA
GUADALCANAL
NOUMEA-GUADALCANAL 980 MILES
INDIAN OCEAN
Darwin
CORAL SEA
NEW CALEDONIA
Nou
AUSTRALIA
Brisbane
Perth
Sydney
SOUT
Melbourne
Au
Welli
NEW ZEALAND

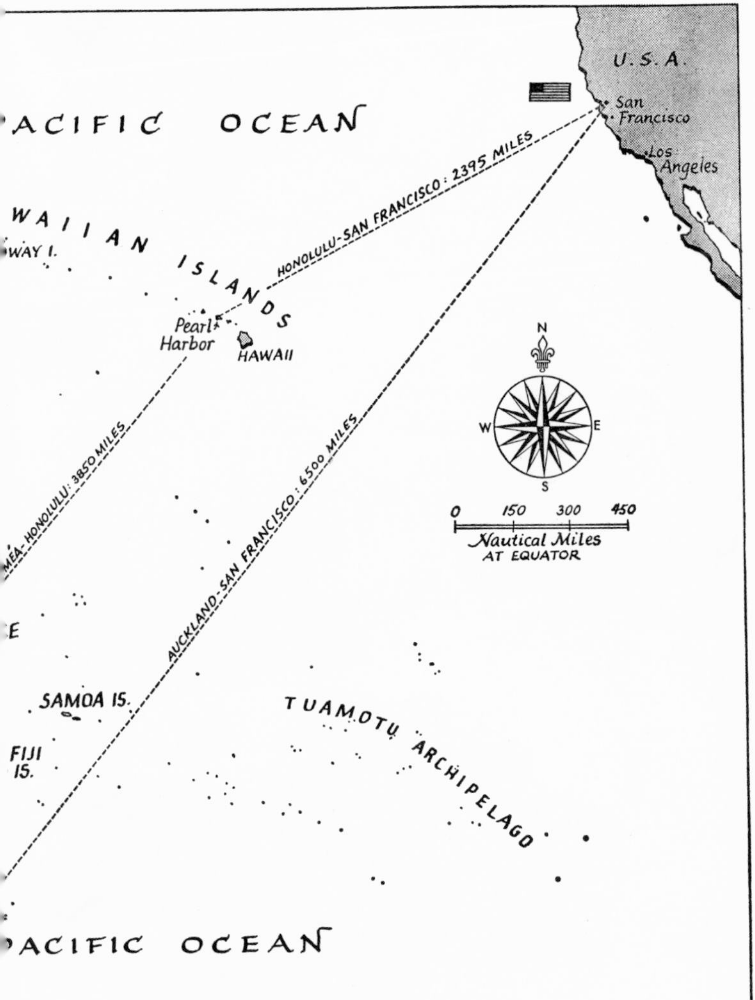

U.S.A.

San Francisco

Los Angeles

ACIFIC OCEAN

WAIIAN ISLANDS

WAY I.

HONOLULU-SAN FRANCISCO : 2395 MILES

Pearl Harbor

HAWAII

N

W

E

S

0 150 300 450

Nautical Miles
AT EQUATOR

MÉA-HONOLULU: 3850 MILES

AUCKLAND-SAN FRANCISCO : 6500 MILES

E

SAMOA IS.

FIJI IS.

TUAMOTU ARCHIPELAGO

ACIFIC OCEAN

CHAPTER ONE

Operation "Watchtower" En Route

AUGUST 6, 1942

One

1

As it had for several days, the sky over the South Pacific in the Solomon Islands area hung gray and gloomy on Thursday, August 6, 1942. The sea was choppy. Somewhere beyond the horizon, lightning marked a tropical squall.

Rolling patches of mist clung to the water's edge. At times the mist thickened into fog dense enough to block out the 75 ships of a northbound U.S. convoy.

The heavy overcast was both an annoyance and a blessing. While the ships had to reduce speed, they were concealed from roving Japanese search planes and submarines. Under cover of the fog the three aircraft carriers, one battleship, 14 cruisers, numerous destroyers, oilers, tankers, cargo, and transport vessels were able to sail undetected toward their destination, a 25-mile-wide, 90-mile-long island called Guadalcanal, the largest of the Solomon Islands.

Only eight months after the Japanese attack on Pearl Harbor, the United States was launching its first offensive in the Pacific War as a naval task force escorted about 15 transports carrying the 11,000-man U.S. 1st Marine Division on a mission officially labeled Operation "Watchtower."

In August, 1942, the 1st Division was the only one in the Marine Corps at combat strength. However, few of its personnel had ever been in battle. Most were recent graduates of boot camp or Officers Candidate School. But because it was the only force available, the green division had been chosen to seize Guadalcanal, and its neighboring islands, Tulagi, Florida, Gavutu, and Tanambogo.

Sending untried troops against Japanese veterans, the victors of many battles, was risky enough. But the hazards were heightened for the U.S. because the aircraft carriers supporting the invasion—the *Saratoga, Wasp,* and *Enterprise*—were the only flattops the U.S. Navy could muster in the South Pacific, while the battleship *North Carolina* was the sole American capital ship for a thousand miles.

Anxiety about Operation "Watchtower" reached from the White House in Washington, D.C., to the officers directly responsible for its success.

Rear Admiral Richmond Kelly Turner, commanding the transport and cargo ships, was worried. Each of his vessels was packed to the gunwales with men and equipment. The responsibility for landing the Marines and unloading tons of weapons, ammunition, fuel, medicines, tanks, jeeps, and rations rested with him.

Small wonder that his bushy brows were drawn together in a deep frown. Putting the men and supplies ashore on a strange island in uncharted waters was a crushing task. He paced the bridge of his flagship, the transport *McCawley,* mentally wrestling with the innumerable problems that had been plaguing him since the convoy had sailed from a mid-ocean rendezvous about 400 miles south of the Fiji Islands on July 26.

Like Turner, Vice Admiral Frank Jack Fletcher, aboard the aircraft carrier *Saratoga,* was also troubled. The veteran of the Coral Sea and Midway naval battles fretted over the safety of his flattops. In the Coral Sea fighting he had lost the carrier *Lexington* and, at Midway, the *Yorktown.*

The U.S. Navy could not afford to lose any carriers on this mission, but Fletcher knew the enemy would be coming after his ships with planes and submarines once the battle got underway.

Even the thought of a carrier being sunk by enemy action brought cold sweat to the admiral's forehead. He was in a quandary. He had to protect the convoy without endangering his ships. Few combat naval officers would have cared to be in Fletcher's place.

The other ranking officers were Rear Admiral Leigh Noyes, who commanded the planes of the Air Support

Force, and Rear Admiral V. A. C. Crutchley, British Royal Navy (several warships were Australian), in charge of the cruisers and destroyers shepherding the transports and freighters. They, too, were deeply concerned.

It was an uneasy time for any man in a position of authority, particularly Major General Alexander Vandegrift, Commanding Officer (CO) of the 1st Marine Division. He went sleepless night after night checking and rechecking the battle plans. A longtime Marine, Vandegrift knew victory was won by sound preparation. Should Operation "Watchtower" fail, it must not happen because he had overlooked the slightest detail.

Those most directly involved with whatever lay ahead seemed least perturbed. The Marines who were going to do the fighting passed the days on shipboard resting, reading, sleeping, gambling, and arguing. They sang and cracked jokes, these brash, cocksure youths who wore rumpled green Marine fatigues.

But the young warriors were not as carefree as they seemed. Each man secretly wondered how he would behave under fire. It was easy to swagger, brag, and put up a front by claiming an eagerness for combat; but when a man was alone, doubts gnawed at him. It was easy to plunge a bayonet into a straw dummy during boot camp training; but what was it like to sink cold steel into a man's body? Shooting at a target was fun; but how did one fire at a man in cold blood?

Years later, a Marine who had been on one of the transports and had taken part in the Guadalcanal campaign, could remember: "It's only the first time you feel bad about killing a man. Maybe even the second and the third, too. After that, killing becomes impersonal—a nasty job you must do. Anyway, there's no time for morality in war; you shoot first or you're dead!"

But even the most sensitive Marine did not brood long over the coming struggle. Killing and dying were not yet realities. And Marines didn't shy at shadows; these were hand-picked fighting men—the best in the U.S.A. Each Leatherneck was a volunteer, scornful of the Navy's drafted "swabbies" and the Army's conscript "dogfaces."

"A Marine's half-sailor, half-soldier, and all scrapper!" they bragged.

The almost unbroken string of Japanese victories since the start of the Pacific War did not impress these headstrong boys (the average Marine was less than 20 years old). Nor were they awed by the foe's reputation in battle.

Their attitude toward the Japanese was demonstrated during a shipboard orientation lecture in which a captain vividly described the enemy's fighting tactics. After telling his men about the Japanese soldier's skill in the jungle, his craftiness, his endurance, and his cruel treatment of prisoners, the officer concluded, "You men can see what you'll be facing—fanatics who'll gladly die for the Emperor." He studied the earnest young faces of his audience. "Now, tell me what you'd do if a Jap popped up right in front of you?"

"Kick him in the teeth!" the Marines roared in concert.

A former Marine recalled how his unit made ready for combat. "All over the deck you heard a scraping noise as the guys sharpened their knives and bayonets on whetstones. Nobody looked forward to using steel on the Nips, but we wanted our hardware ready in case. Besides, it gave us something to do."

There were also more important chores to perform than honing knives and bayonets. Down in the airless holds, work parties loaded cargo nets with small arms ammunition and artillery shells. Straining winches hauled 75-mm and 105-mm guns topside for unloading onto the invasion beach; spare parts, barbed wire, jeeps, rations, and a thousand other items were brought on deck.

As the labor details sweated at that hard toil, crews checked .50 and .30 caliber machine guns. Men swabbed clean their '03 Springfield rifles. Mortars were made spick-and-span, packstraps and ammunition belts adjusted; the ritual of those preparing for battle.

All through the convoy, men were busy. Mechanics on the flattops went over the Dauntless (SBD) dive bombers, the Avenger (TBF) torpedo-bombers, and Wildcat (F4F) fighters. These would soon be paving a way for the landings with bombing and strafing runs.

Gun crews in the turrets of the *North Carolina,* the

cruisers, and the destroyers made last-minute adjustments; shells were piled in magazines; the ships stripped for action. Gunnery officers inspected firing systems; Damage Control squads examined fire-fighting equipment. Blinker lights flicked on and off as Admiral Fletcher sent orders from ship to ship.

The tropical night closed around the American fleet. Marines leaned against railings and stared moodily into the darkness. Few spoke, for there was nothing left to be said. Perhaps in that private time, even the toughest Leatherneck wondered whether this was destined to be his last night on earth.

2

Operation "Watchtower" had been born in February, 1942. It had originated with the U.S. Chief of Naval Operations (CNO), Admiral Ernest King, and in its first draft made no mention of Guadalcanal. King's plan called only for the occupation of Tulagi and her neighbors, Florida, Gavutu, and Tanambogo. Tulagi had a fine harbor, and it was hoped that it, with the other islands, would provide anchorages and sea-plane bases for an eventual drive on the great Japanese air, navy, and army depot at Rabaul, on New Britain Island, 600 miles to the northwest.

Tulagi and the adjacent islands also could serve as the

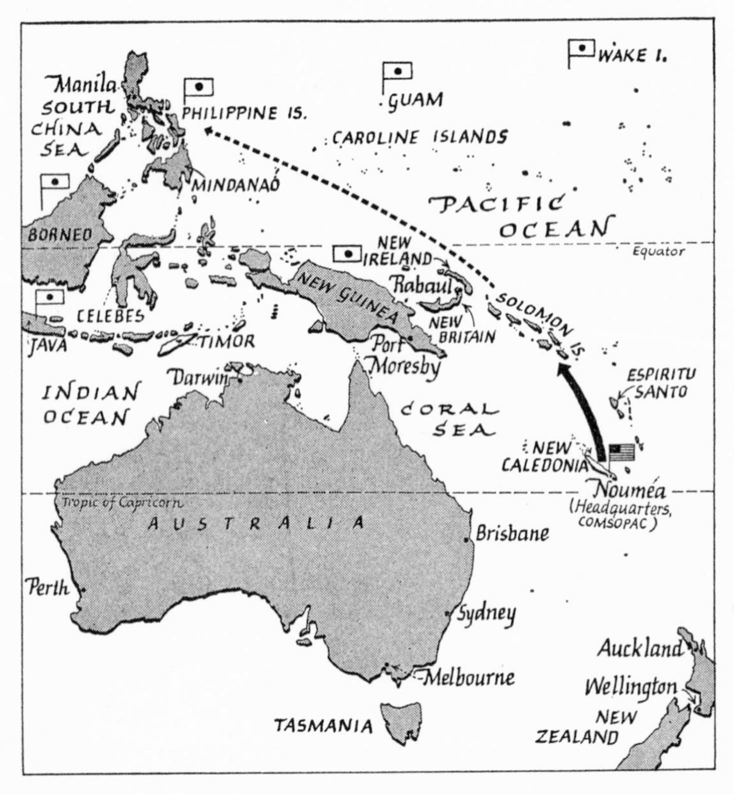

TARGET OF OPERATION "WATCHTOWER"—THE SOLOMONS

springboard for an American counterattack in the Pacific aimed at retaking the Philippines. "We must have Tulagi," declared General Douglas MacArthur. "It is the first step along the road back to Manila."

The U.S. Joint Chiefs of Staff approved Operation "Watchtower" and wheels began turning for the project. At that time (February, 1942), the Japanese had not yet made any move in the Solomon Islands. They already ruled much of the Pacific. The Rising Sun flag flew over Singapore, Malaya, the Philippines, Java, Borneo, Wake, Guam, New Ireland, and New Britain. From Rabaul they menaced New Guinea and Australia. The Solomons did not fall into Japanese control until May, 1942.

Fetid and disease-ridden, the Solomon Islands ran southeast of Rabaul in two columns over 600 miles long. A wide, deep-water passage, New Georgia Sound, known as the Slot, separated the double ranks of the Solomons. Choiseul, Santa Isabel, and Malaita were to the northeast, while New Georgia, Guadalcanal, and San Cristobal stood to the southwest. Dozens of smaller islands, such as Tulagi, Florida, Russell, Rendova, Vella Lavella, and Buka, dotted the ocean between.

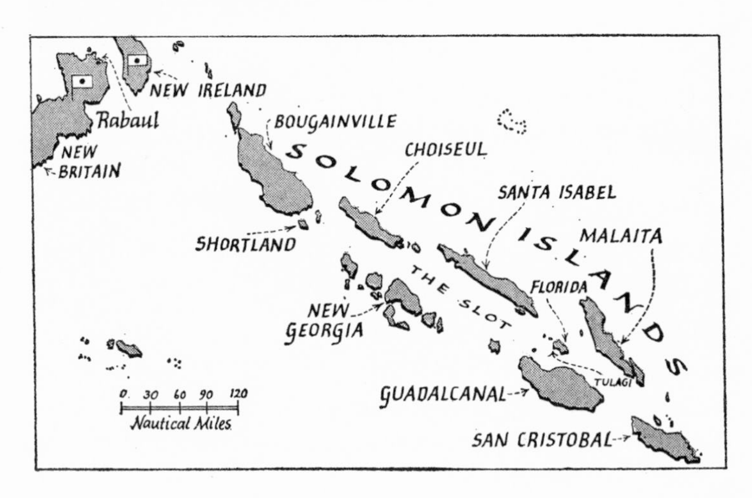

Each island, large or small, was plagued by malarial mosquitoes that bred in swamps and bogs; only Tulagi was comparatively free of the disease. *Kunai* grass, rising to heights of seven feet, gave the deceptive impression of lush pasture land from the distance. Up close each blade of *kunai* proved tough and fibrous, with saw-tooth edges that could rip a man's flesh.

Here, in these equatorial islands, rain-drenched and steaming hot the year around, civilization had made few inroads over the four hundred years since a young Spanish adventurer, Don Alvaro Mendaña, accidentally came upon the islands while searching for the legendary King Solomon's Gold Mine. He named the newly found lands for that ancient wise ruler of Israel.

Even as late as 1942, Solomon Islanders were scarcely affected by events in the outside world. British-ruled, the islands slumbered in the sun. From time to time, Catholic or Protestant missionaries ventured among the natives and achieved some success in converting them to forms of Christianity.

Tulagi, the provincial capital, boasted a few stores, a palm-thatched church, a radio station, and a cricket field. At the outbreak of the Pacific War, the Australians stationed a squadron of flying boats in Gavutu Harbor near Tulagi. But Japanese bombers started striking in January, 1942. At the end of April, an enemy naval force was reported heading for Tulagi. The Australians ordered the island evacuated and the Japanese won a foothold in the Solomons without firing a shot.

The enemy seizure of Tulagi, May 2, jolted the men working on Operation "Watchtower" which had been proceeding at a good clip. In March, units of the 1st Marine Division had sailed for New Zealand from their training camp at New River, North Carolina. Not even General Vandegrift knew the details of the mission. He had been advised only that his men were to spearhead the first U.S. offensive of the Pacific War.

The general believed he would have at least six months in New Zealand to complete training his troops before leading them in an offensive action.

This respite was denied him when the Japanese on Tulagi took steps that altered both the timetable and the target of Operation "Watchtower." These changes now brought Guadalcanal into the picture.

Separated from Tulagi by a three-mile-wide body of water called Sealark Channel, Guadalcanal remained untouched by the Japanese except for occasional patrols. But in July, an Australian reconnaissance plane noticed a 13-ship enemy convoy landing men and supplies at Lunga Point on Guadalcanal.

Continued daily observation revealed that the enemy was building an airfield near Lunga Point—and making good progress.

This intelligence stirred concern among the Americans.

From the Guadalcanal airfield, enemy bombers could hit U.S. installations throughout the South Pacific. The American naval, air, and military installations on Espiritu Santo, Efate, Nouméa, the Fijis, and New Zealand would be subjected to attack from the air. U.S. ships supplying these bases would be endangered and the American position in the Southwest Pacific severely menaced if the Guadalcanal airfield was permitted to become operational.

Something had to be done at once. Major General Vandegrift was summoned from New Zealand to Nouméa where the Commanding Officer of the South Pacific (Comsopac), Vice Admiral Robert Ghormley, had his headquarters. He handed Vandegrift a sheet of typewritten paper which read:

> FROM: CNO, WASHINGTON, D.C.
> TO: COMSOPAC, NOUMÉA, NEW CALEDONIA
>
> You will seize, occupy, and defend Tulagi and adjacent positions (Guadalcanal and Florida Islands and Santa Cruz Islands) in order to deny those areas to the enemy and to provide U.S. bases for further offensive operations. . . .

After perusing the orders, Vandegrift glanced up at Ghormley. "Sir, who is to do the seizing?" he asked.

"You, General," Ghormley replied.

For once in his Marine Corps career, General Vandegrift

was taken aback. His division was far from combat readiness. Its units were still scattered: the 1st Regiment was at sea en route to New Zealand from San Francisco; the 7th Regiment, encamped outside Wellington, New Zealand; the other regiments and supporting groups that comprised the division were either traveling or about to board ships in various U.S. ports of embarkation.

The 1st Division had never even conducted maneuvers as a body. Surely, Comsopac knew this. While Vandegrift made no protest, his expression must have given away his thoughts, for Ghormley eyed him sympathetically.

"I'm sorry to throw this at you, Vandegrift. I know your division's green—but it's the only force available at this time," he said.

"We'll do it, sir," Vandegrift assured him. "When is D-Day?"

"August first."

Vandegrift pursed his lips. That gave him only a little more than a month's time to assemble the division, gather supplies, and mount the invasion. On the surface it was impossible.

"When you've been in the Corps all your life, you learn that nothing is impossible," Vandegrift commented later. "Some jobs are more difficult, that's all. I had my orders and proceeded to carry them out."

Vandegrift flew back to his New Zealand camp and broke the news to his staff. "We were shaken by the package the Old Man dropped," an aide recalled. "But we worked around the clock and the general was with us every step. Somehow, everything that had to be done was done."

The hardest job was to gather information about Guadalcanal. In the entire world, only a few hundred people knew anything about Guadalcanal or any of the other Solomon Islands. The seas around them were virtually uncharted. In fact, the most up-to-date hydrographic charts dated back to 1910.

According to an Australian government map maker, "In my twenty years on this job, nobody ever asked for new charts of Guadalcanal. After all, until now, who cared about a pesthole like that?"

It fell upon Lt. Colonel Frank B. Goettge, the Division Intelligence Officer (D-2), to gather the needed information. Goettge, an able, energetic officer, made aerial reconnaissances of Guadalcanal and Tulagi, interviewed planters and missionaries who had been there, and gathered data from the so-called "coastwatchers," daring volunteers who hid themselves in the occupied Solomon Islands to spy on the Japanese and report their findings by radio. In a short time, D-2 had collected enough material for General Vandegrift to draw up a tentative battle plan.

It was decided that the Marines were to force landings at five points. The 1st and 5th Marines (Marine regiments were always referred to as "Marines" and designated by number) would hit Guadalcanal's northern beaches at a point roughly ten miles from the center of the 90-mile-long island. Tulagi was to be taken by the 1st Marine Raider Battalion; another Marine battalion would secure Florida; Gavutu and Tanambogo were left to the 1st Marine Parachute Battalion fighting as infantry.

By July 22, only two days after the 1st Marine Division had been reunited in New Zealand, Vandegrift's men were at sea bound for a rendezvous with the naval escort forces off the Fiji Islands.

While sailing to the Fijis, Vandegrift was advised by radio that D-Day has been pushed back to August 7, granting him an extra week to polish his battle plans. But the good news was seasoned by bad. At the rendezvous area, Admiral Fletcher informed Vandegrift that the aircraft carriers would remain in the invasion zone no longer than three days.

Fletcher refused to expose his flattops more than 72 hours because, according to Naval Intelligence, the enemy had five carriers and a fleet of fast battleships at Rabaul, plus numerous bombers. The Admiral promised to give air cover during the most critical periods of the invasion and then withdraw. However, the U.S. Navy was not going to abandon the Marines; warships under Admiral Turner were committed to remain as long as needed.

This afforded slight comfort to Vandegrift. Turner's heaviest ships were cruisers and the general saw his division stranded on "God-forsaken Guadalcanal without aerial support and only the cruisers to protect us against Jap planes and battlewagons. You can be sure it wasn't a cheery prospect. I raised a fuss to the top brass, but no one paid attention. I had no alternative except to get on with the job. . . . I did not tell my people about Fletcher's decision . . . I figured they'd find out for themselves, soon enough. . . ."

3

Since his men never had engaged in landing exercises, General Vandegrift hoped to hold maneuvers on Koro Island in the Fijis. Putting a division ashore from ships was both complex and involved. The men had to climb down cargo nets slung over the sides of the transports into landing craft bobbing on the water far below. This took practice —but landing the men was only part of the problem.

Once the troops had "hit the beach," difficulties really began. Supplies had to be hauled in; everything from shoes and rations to matches and tanks. Only hard training could prepare non-coms and officers for traffic control on the landing areas—otherwise the invasion beaches would wind up in a welter of men, machines, and merchandise.

The general wanted to hold landing, loading, and unloading exercises on Koro, but as one of his staff officers put it, "Somebody had goofed in picking that place for a training ground." The coral reefs that ringed Koro were so sharp that they ripped the bottoms out of the landing craft.

As a result, instead of full-scale practice in "hitting the beach," the Marines merely scrambled down the sides of the ships, dropped into the Higgins Boats (landing craft), rode through the surf to the coral reefs, and went back to the ships. This was hardly the preparation Vandegrift wanted for his men.

"We ran up and down the cargo nets lugging full combat gear," a 1st Marines officer said, "then taxied up to Koro without ever setting foot on dry land. I couldn't see the sense to it, but we kept on all day long, for three days."

On the morning of July 31, two destroyers led the large convoy away from the Fijis in a north-northwesterly direction. After a week, the ships were nearing their destination. The night of August 6–7 was moonless. Rain-fat clouds waddled across the sky; thunderheads marked rain squalls. It was hot and humid.

Belowdecks in the troop holds men tossed sleeplessly on the sweaty, five-tiered bunks. For them nothing remained but to wait, think, and perhaps pray. . . .

At 0200 (2:00 A.M.) the night watch sighted Cape Esperance at the northwestern tip of Guadalcanal. The vessels glided silently through calm waters; the weather had cleared and the moon was bright in a star-studded tropical sky.

Lookouts soon noted the cone-shaped bulk of Savo Island, a slag heap of volcanic rock, rising out of the water like some prehistoric monster, at the western approach to Sealark Channel.

The convoy split into two sections at Savo Island. Those ships carrying the 1st and 5th Marines swung out to pass between Savo and the landing beach on Guadalcanal. The rest of the vessels turned north above Savo and then eastwards for the run to Tulagi, Florida, Gavutu, and Tanambogo.

THE BATTLEGROUND

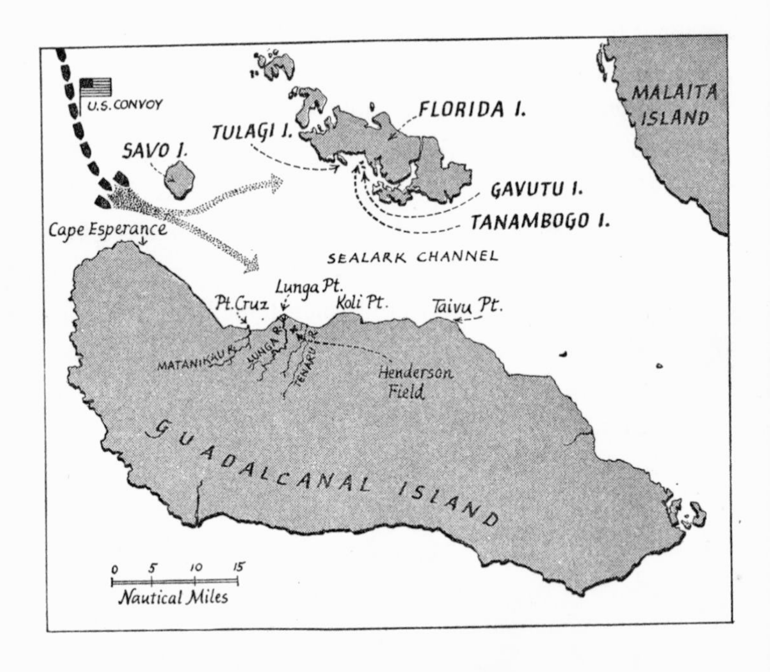

By 0647 (6:47 A.M.) all ships were at invasion stations. The troops were roused and sent to breakfast fully armed. "They fed us beans," a Marine remembered. "Beans! A guy in the death house gets a banquet before going to the electric chair and we had beans! I swore to myself that when the war was over, I'd never eat beans again!"

After gulping down their unappetizing breakfast, the assault units clambered topside up the steep iron gangway ladders. The Marines lined up on deck in full combat gear and blinked in the bright sunshine; it was a perfect day, blue sky arching over blue-green waters that rippled gently against the hulls of the ships. Below, Higgins Boats circled, leaving a frothy wake behind.

"The boys looked pale in that morning sun; I couldn't decide whether their color came from being cooped up so long in the hold or because we were all so scared. But there wasn't enough time to worry about such things. We hadn't been up on deck ten minutes before the Navy guns began to pound the shore," a Marine recollected.

On Tulagi, Gavutu, and Tanambogo, the 8-inch guns of the cruisers set roaring blazes; great clouds of smoke darkened the sky over Guadalcanal. Destroyers raced in close to blast enemy positions at pointblank range.

As the pre-invasion barrage reached its crescendo Wildcat fighters and Dauntless bombers barreled in from the open sea where the *Wasp, Saratoga,* and *Enterprise* were cruising. The carrier planes made unopposed strikes, strafing and bombing at will. It was a Pearl Harbor in reverse; now the Japanese had been taken unawares.

On both sides of Sealark Channel, the Japanese snapped awake when the first U.S. shells exploded, to stare incredulously at the channel crowded with American ships.

Four Kawanishi 97 (Mavis) sea-planes riding at their moorings in Tulagi Harbor were attacked by strafing Wildcats. The Mavises burst into flames. One tried to take off but was downed by a cruiser's anti-aircraft (AA) guns.

The Marines watched the bombardment from their debarkation stations. "It looked good. The Nips were taking a real pasting. It must have been hell on their end. They didn't even fire a shot in return," a Marine sergeant said.

After pounding the enemy positions for three quarters of an hour with shells and bombs, Major General Vandegrift nodded to his signal officer. Moments later, the command, "Marines, board your landing craft!" was resounding from the loudspeakers on the transports. Squad after squad started down the cargo nets to the waiting Higgins Boats.

The descent to the landing craft went without a hitch. "It's like a training drill," remarked a sailor aboard the transport *Hunter Liggett*.

Shortly before 0800 (8:00 A.M.) the Higgins Boats, now filled with Marines, fanned out into a wide-spread line and streaked toward the enemy-held shores.

CHAPTER TWO

Operation "Watchtower" The Landings

AUGUST 7, 1942

Two

1

With roaring motors, the Higgins Boats sped over the glassy water, throwing up creamy bow waves, and leaving a churning wake. The helmsmen steered the landing craft to an indentation on the shore line between Lunga and Koli Points. D-2 had selected this sector—a 1,600 yard stretch bounded on the west by the Matanikau River and on the east by the Tenaru River—as the place most suitable for the landings.

From the sea, Guadalcanal seemed like a tropical paradise. She was green and verdant, her beaches white in the sun. The men in the Higgins Boats could only note the island's external beauty. They did not then know that beyond the beaches Guadalcanal held foul swamps and bogs where crocodiles slithered in slimy lagoons. The Marines still had to learn about the rats, carrion birds, malarial mosquitoes, poisonous snakes, and monstrous crabs; the squirming, crawling, and flying jungle creatures.

As they came closer, the invaders noticed a strange odor rising from the island—a smell of rotting matter emanating out of jungles where vegetation had been decaying for centuries. In the jungles muddy trails twisted through growth so thick that sunlight had never penetrated.

Narrow paths led to open areas where the sun beat down upon clusters of crude huts. In these "villages" naked children played amid filth and offal. Mangy dogs nosed through garbage heaps. Natives, suffering from yaws, dengue, trachoma, and other diseases lived and died on Guadalcanal as had the people of the Stone Age. The rains came day or night without warning. The constant dampness brought on a variety of skin diseases. Guadalcanal was riddled with its own cancerous decay.

At 0910 (9:10 A.M.) the American landing craft grated onto the sandbars. Marines leaped off in waist-deep water to wade ashore and drop panting upon the hot sand.

None of the men storming ashore expected the landings to come off so easily. "Somebody's going to get hurt!" the Leathernecks had predicted. In the Marine Corps such talk meant the troops anticipated heavy casualties.

But when 1st (Red) and 3rd (Blue) battalions, 5th Marines, sloshed onto the beach they faced little resistance. A machine gun or two chattered briefly. Here and there enemy rifles cracked. Not one Marine was hit. After putting up feeble opposition, the defending Japanese fled to the jungle and disappeared in the thick underbrush. Both battalions of the 5th Marines pressed inland and swung westward to the Lunga River where they came upon the main Japanese camp which housed the 1,700 man labor force working on the airfield.

There was plenty of evidence that the enemy had left in a hurry. The Marines found bowls filled with rice and cups of morning tea on the long tables in the open air mess hall.

As the 5th Marines advanced, overrunning Japanese installations including work shacks, an ice house, and a radio transmitter station, the 1st Marines landed behind them and Beach Red was soon teeming with more than 10,000 men.

Red, White, and Blue battalions, 1st Marines, immediately pushed off the beach. Red Battalion seized the undefended airfield and found it to be nearly completed with hangars, machine shops, sheds, bomb shelters, and a 3,600 foot long runway. (The Marines named the captured strip Henderson Field for Major Lofton Henderson, a Marine pilot who had crash-dived his bomber onto an enemy cruiser during the Battle of Midway, to win a posthumous award of the Congressional Medal of Honor.)

Red Battalion dug in around the airfield. White and Blue Battalions marched south into the jungle toward a high hill called Grassy Knoll. Enemy gun positions there could easily bombard Henderson Field. For this reason, General Vandegrift wanted to seize the high ground.

On the map, Grassy Knoll seemed to loom just beyond the airfield, possibly less than a mile away. It proved to be five miles distant, through some of the worst jungle on Guadalcanal. But the 1st Marines plunged into that tangle of *kunai* grass and foliage, expecting to be atop Grassy Knoll in a short time.

Instead of a quick advance, the Marines floundered on slopes slick with mud. Ascending a hill was bad; but getting down was misery. The footing was so unsure that men went sliding headfirst as though on a toboggan run. Progress was just as difficult on level ground. Platoons disappeared amid clusters of *kunai* grass which closed in like a living wall of green barbed wire. Only after wearisome hacking with machetes could a path be hewn.

Units became disorganized; companies blundered apart; even squads lost contact. No one was sure whether friend or foe moved in the bush beside him. The jungle was so dense that a man did not know what lay five yards to either side.

As they stumbled onward, the Marines constantly expected a clash with the enemy. Surely, the foe lurked in the shadows, behind the next tree, or at the edge of a bog. At times, jittery Marines, hearing movement to the left or right, triggered a burst of tommy gun or rifle fire into the underbrush only to hear an indignant American voice shout, "Hold your fire, you damned fool!"

Miraculously, this trigger-happy activity caused no casualties. So the grueling march to Grassy Knoll went on. Suddenly the trail led across a swift, icy stream that tumbled furiously down a steep ravine. Some flung themselves face down into the freshet and gulped like thirsty animals. One anxious officer tried to keep his men from drinking.

"Don't, boys!" he cried. "It may be poisoned!"

"Come on, sir," a Marine said, wiping his dripping face with a sweat-stained sleeve. "The Japs can't poison a whole river!"

All day they marched, more like rabble than disciplined troops. Every Marine knew about flank guards, scouts and patrols ahead, and connecting files between squads and companies. But the training manuals had not been written for the Guadalcanal jungle. It was impossible to maintain proper military order.

The march turned into a test of individual endurance. Later, after the Marines had gained jungle experience, they seldom repeated the mistakes that had been made on that terrible trek to Grassy Knoll.

"We were lucky," Lt. Col. Edwin Pollock, CO, White Battalion, later recalled. "The Japs could've wiped us out if they'd had any kind of defensive set-up. As it was, we were given a second chance, but only because the Nips had grown so overconfident they didn't feel it necessary to prepare against an invasion. The Jap looked at us with contempt back in '42 and by the time he saw his mistake we were at his throat. . . ."

Despite the hard going, nothing dampened the Leathernecks' morale or stifled their humor. On the way to Grassy Knoll, two panting machine gunners, bending double under the weight of barrel, tripod, and ammunition, struggled up a path in ankle deep mud.

"Why the devil does the Old Man want Grassy Knoll, anyway?" grunted one man.

"It's the only place with a view, that's why!" his companion responded.

"So what?"

"So where else're they goin' to put up the officers' club?" the second gunner snorted.

White and Blue battalions were called to a halt at nightfall. Stragglers lurched in as companies, platoons, and squads regrouped and the Marines dug foxholes for their first night in the jungle.

The cries of birds were raucous and frightening; every sound was amplified and nervous sentries fired into the darkness. Almost all night long a torrential rain fell and, in the momentary intervals between downpours, swarms of mosquitoes tormented the weary men huddled under ponchos that did not keep them dry and mosquito netting which gave no protection from insect bites.

The night dragged past. At daybreak, bleary-eyed Marines with swollen faces and wet uniforms made a cold breakfast of K-rations and again moved out in the direction of Grassy Knoll which loomed mockingly before them. By mid-morning they had scrambled to its crest and stood looking down across the green hell through which they had passed. To the north they could see Henderson Field and the beach beyond.

There were neither traces of Japanese gun positions on Grassy Knoll, nor of anyone's ever having set foot there. This information was radioed back to the Division Command Post (CP) and the troops were ordered back to Beach Red. The long march had been without purpose except to determine that no enemy was on the Knoll.

"We didn't have to make that back-breaking hike," a disgruntled Marine said. "The brass should've figured out the Japs had more sense than to want Grassy Knoll."

With much grumbling and griping the battalions started for Beach Red. On the way, they heard heavy gunfire coming from across Sealark Channel where Tulagi was located. Obviously, a fight was raging there. The enemy was defending Tulagi. But where were the Japanese on Guadalcanal? Were they going to give up without a battle?

The Guadalcanal Marines listened to the sounds of the battle. They had confidence in their comrades on Tulagi: the 1st Marine Raider Battalion, under Colonel Merritt Edson, who was known as "Red Mike" for his carrot-colored hair. The unit fighting on Gavutu and Tanambogo, adjacent to Tulagi, was the 1st Marine Parachute Battalion, a tough and reliable bunch.

"There was nothing we could do except sit tight," a Guadalcanal Marine remembered. "I think, at the time, we envied the Raiders and Paratroopers. They were in a battle while we still had to fire a shot in anger."

But as the sun rose higher, the Guadalcanal Marines had no time to think about missing a fight. They had a lot to do that had to be done fast. The transports needed unloading and soon long lines of Marines were toiling in a human chain passing cases of rations, munitions, and medical supplies ashore to a background of machine guns, rifles, and mortars over on Tulagi.

Beach Red soon became a jumble of boxes, crates, moving vehicles, sweating men, and whining motors. Tractors dragged 75-mm guns through the sand. Amphibious tanks splashed, growled, and roared ashore from the landing barges. Out in Sealark Channel dozens of small boats zigzagged among the freighters and warships.

Although the work parties toiled hard they could not get the ships unloaded fast enough and nervous cargomasters sent hurry calls to General Vandegrift for more men. The Marine CO dared not release any more line troops for labor details. He had to be ready for a Japanese counterthrust at any time and any place.

The men worked at top speed until noon when they paused for a breather after scores of them had passed out from exertion in the blazing sun. The weary stevedores dragged themselves into the shaded jungle for a rest, but found none. Just as the last Marines straggled off the beach, the enemy struck his first blow on Guadalcanal.

Twenty Japanese dive bombers and an equal number of torpedo bombers suddenly swept into sight, flying low over Sealark Channel. As they appeared AA guns on ship and shore opened a terrifying barrage. A row of Nakajima 97 (Kate) torpedo-bombers speeding toward the cargo ships ran head-on into the curtain of American lead. Twelve Kates fell spinning from the sky. Only one torpedo-bomber got through. She loosed a "tin fish" and scored a hit on the U.S.S. *Jarvis,* a destroyer, only an instant before being shot down. (The *Jarvis* suffered severe damage and was sunk by enemy aircraft a day or so later, going down with all hands.)

As the Kates were being annihilated, Aichi 99 (Val) dive-bombers plummeted out of the blue, apparently expecting to take the Americans by surprise. However, the Japanese were caught in a neatly sprung U.S. trap. Wildcat fighters from the *Wasp* had been hovering overhead nearly half an hour awaiting the arrival of the Japanese planes.

The Val pilots, diving into the AA fire, were so intent on bombing the ships below that they never noticed the Wildcats screeching down on them. The enemy was slaughtered by streams of .50 caliber machine gun bullets pouring

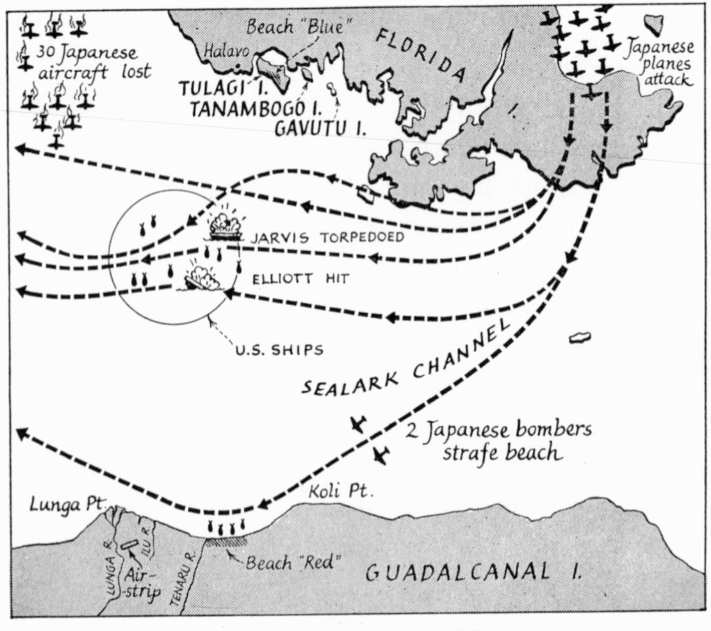

THE ENEMY STRIKES

from the Wildcats. Few Vals escaped, and only one managed to score on a transport.

The Japanese plane, ablaze and out of control, plunged into the open hold of the *George F. Elliott*. The ship caught fire and after burning for many hours went under with all the supplies of a Marine battalion.

The raid ended quickly. It had been a costly one for the Japanese. The foe lost at least 30 aircraft at a price of damage to the *Jarvis* and the *Elliott*. The main purpose of the enemy had been foiled. The supplies on the beach were untouched and all the cargo ships unscathed.

This victory did not come about by accident. At 0850 (8:50 A.M.) the Japanese planes had been spotted by a coastwatcher who radioed Comsopac at Nouméa: "Forty Nip bombers going southeast." Comsopac flashed the word to Turner and Fletcher and the whole U.S. invasion force was alerted to the raid.

When the attack ended, the work parties, elated by the beating handed the enemy, rushed to their tasks with such will that the clutter on the beach began to disappear as supplies were hauled inland to hastily prepared storage depots.

By mid-day August 8, the situation seemed "well in hand" for the Marines on Guadalcanal. But over on the harbor islands—Tulagi, Gavutu, and Tanambogo—where little difficulty had been expected, different conditions prevailed. Both Edson's Raiders and the Paratroopers commanded by Major Robert Williams were in trouble.

"The Japs on Tulagi, Gavutu, and Tanambogo gave us a good preview of what we had to face later in the Pacific War at Tarawa, Iwo Jima, Okinawa, and Saipan," a Marine intelligence officer noted.

2

Boot-shaped Tulagi Island was a far more suitable setting for a South Seas moving picture than a battleground. Green and placid, Tulagi overlooked her splendid harbor drowsily. But her calm appearance was deceptive. The Japanese had masterfully fortified the tip of the boot. The defenders squeezed in among the rocks that jutted up in that part of the island. They had emplaced machine guns, mortars, and automatic weapons to cover the beach and the concrete boat landing ramps.

On D-Day (August 7) U.S. Naval gunfire plastered Tulagi's rocky slopes with high explosive (HE) shells. The missiles set many fires along the shore line and pulverized the landing ramps. Most houses within range were shattered and enemy craft moored at the beach had been splintered, but the U.S. guns could not dislodge the foe from his prepared positions.

During the bombardment, the Japanese crawled into the numerous caves that pockmarked Tulagi's hills. When the ships ceased firing, the Mikado's men rushed out of hiding places to their machine guns and mortars and blasted away at the Raiders landing from Higgins Boats.

"We got ashore without trouble. I guess the barrage had shook up the Japs because their shooting was awful. Luckily for us they fired too high and their mortars were way off target. But we had a darn good taste of how it felt to be shot at," a Raider non-com remembered.

The Raiders were followed ashore by Red Battalion, 5th Marines, who swarmed over the northwestern sector of the island as Edson's men tried to clean out enemy resistance at the tip of the boot.

When the Raiders began to advance among the rocks

and trees the enemy opened a galling sniper fire. Japanese suicide squads hid amid the rubble of houses or dug in under the roots of tall trees. They fired down from tree tops and took cover in the gaping holes the naval shells had gouged out.

Marines began to fall and cries of "Corpsman!" and "Stretcher bearer!" were frequently heard. The corpsmen, whose Red Cross brassards made targets for the snipers, went unflinchingly under fire to aid the wounded.

The Leathernecks learned about combat quickly. "We were green when we hit the beach but you became a veteran out there fast," a young Marine said.

Fighting from caves, the Japanese rained machine gun bullets and mortar shells on the Marines busy flushing out snipers. A whole Raider company was pinned down by two enemy machine guns poking from narrow-mouthed caves on the crest of one slope.

The Raiders had to inch forward through a field of *kunai* grass and then up the hillside in the face of the spitting guns. After more than an hour of this torturous advance, several Marines came within grenade throwing distance of the machine gun nest.

A Raider who had been the star pitcher of his high school baseball team only brief months before, reared up and pegged a grenade squarely into the cave mouth as bullets kicked up dirt around him. He followed this with another "pineapple" and then another until the guns had been silenced.

"I knew I had to pitch perfect strikes," he later asserted. "The Japs had the bases loaded and nobody out!"

Japanese resistance did not slacken despite the loss of this strongpoint. The Marines were held up at the edge of the cricket field which was set in a valley between two rocky hills. There, the enemy had emplaced a series of machine gun nests dug into the sides of the humpbacked hills. A furious fight raged until dusk at the cricket field.

As daylight waned, the Americans dug in, disgruntled because they had been unable to complete the capture of Tulagi that day. The Raiders prepared to spend their first night on enemy soil. It was a night none of Edson's men was likely to forget.

In the darkness beyond the cricket field, the Yanks, crouching in hastily scooped-out foxholes, could hear the enemy tramping out of the hills. The foe made no attempt to conceal his movements.

"What're they doin'?" a sentry whispered tensely to a comrade.

"Search me, Mac. But no matter what, I'll bet anything they mean to give us a hard time."

The anonymous Marine was right. The "hard time" came in the form of the first *banzai* charge of the war by the Mikado's soldiers against Americans. (*Banzai,* a Japanese cheer used to greet the Emperor, literally means 10,000 years or long life to the Mikado.) The fanatical assault was a last-ditch effort to cut the American lines and drive the Yanks into the sea.

Long before they had come overseas to fight the Japanese, back in boot camp, the Marines had heard scuttlebutt about *banzai* charges from the old hands who had served in China. The boots were filled with graphic descriptions of *sake*-crazed Nipponese hurling themselves against the foe without regard to losses.

"The Japs consider it an honor to die for the Mikado," a Marine sergeant who had been in China explained. He had seen a *banzai* attack launched against a strongly defended Chinese position back in 1937. "The Nips came on screeching and yammering. Nothing stopped 'em. Not machine guns or automatic rifles. That charge was a cross between a Comanche raid and a waterfront brawl. Getting killed didn't bother the Japs. According to *bushido,* a man who gets knocked off in combat is honorable."

Despite all they had heard about Japanese fanaticism, the Tulagi Marines were unprepared for the fury which struck them. For some time, the enemy continued his noisy preparations; then a single red rocket flowered in the August night and the enemy swarmed out of the bush onto the American positions.

They charged in small groups—only ten or fifteen together. The officers waved *samurai* swords. The Japanese came on, firing from the hip and screaming *"Banzai! Banzai!"* or shouting in English, "Yank, you die! Yank, you die!"

As the attack boiled toward them, the Marines gaped in wonder. The enemy was rushing across an open space almost 100 yards wide and covered by rifles, machine guns, and other rapid-fire weapons. It seemed incredible to the Americans that men should be so heedless of their lives, for when the guns opened up, the Japanese fell by scores.

Bullets slowed that crazed attack, but could not stop it. By twos and three, the Japanese slipped into the Marine positions and came to grips with knives and bayonets. Furious hand-to-hand fighting swirled up and down the American perimeter. The foes used pistols, fists, rifle butts, rocks, and fists on each other. In several places the Marine lines were pierced but reserves plugged the gaps.

The enemy regrouped time after time and launched other forays. The combat raged all night. Not until daybreak did the enemy slink off to his caves and leave the ground still in Marine hands.

An American counterattack on August 8 finally broke Japanese resistance on Tulagi, although isolated snipers, hidden in inaccessible caves, were still being hunted months later. Most of the defenders had fought to the death. A few wounded men were taken prisoner and about 30 Japanese swam across the narrow water passage to Florida Island where they disappeared into the jungle.

3

While the fighting on Tulagi was going on, Baker (B) Company, Red Battalion, 2nd Marines, captured Haleta Village on Florida Island without firing a shot. The occupation was complete by 0740 (7:40 A.M.), Friday, August 7.

As Baker Company was having its easy conquest, the 1st Marine Parachute Battalion ran into trouble on tiny Gavutu and Tanambogo. The Japanese there fought with astounding ferocity.

The Paramarines had to drive the foe from every cave and foxhole. As the fighting progressed, the Marines improvised tactics. One officer, Captain Harry Torgerson, tied sticks of dynamite to wooden poles and hurled the explosives into the cave mouths as though they were javelins.

If an aperture was too small, Torgerson would push his lethal package into the enemy's hideout. The dynamite had a five-second fuse and sometimes only an instant separated Torgerson's throw or push from the blast. In that eyewink, he had to leap for safety.

After successfully carrying off several such missions, the backlash of an explosion caught the captain. His men cringed as the officer was flung high into the air.

"He flew head over heels and we thought Torgy was a goner for sure," an eyewitness said. "He hit the ground hard, then pulled himself to his feet. Torgy was the luckiest guy in the world. He didn't get a scratch! All that happened was his trousers got blown off—but that didn't stop him. He stood there without any pants and hollered, 'Damn it! Get me more dynamite!' and went on all day blowing up Nips!"

At 1845 (6:45 P.M.) just as dusk was closing in, Baker Company, 2nd Marines, the outfit that had taken Florida Islands, was loaded onto Higgins Boats and sent to capture Tanambogo. At the time fighting was still raging on Gavutu and Tulagi, but Brigadier General William H. Rupertus, Assistant CO, 1st Marine Division, who was running the Tulagi-Florida-Gavutu-Tanambogo show, decided the moment was right to make his move against Tanambogo. According to Intelligence reports, that little dot of land would be taken easily.

The Higgins Boats carrying Baker Company were making a wide arc to a Tanambogo beach when U.S. destroyers opened up on the island with broadsides from their five-inch guns. Simultaneously, Dauntless (SBD) dive-bombers from Fletcher's carriers gave the Japanese a lambasting. Marines crouching in the landing craft cheered as a bomb blew an enemy three-inch gun emplacement from a hilltop.

The men grinned at the fires burning all over the island; not a single tree was standing; the tall palms had been torn in half by shell splinters. A hit ignited oil drums stored in a dockside warehouse. Flames lit the deepening darkness with an orange-red glow.

"We expected a pushover," a Baker Company platoon leader said. "Oh, man, were we ever wrong!"

When the boats reached a point about 100 yards from the beach a five-inch shell from one of the destroyers fell short and exploded amidst the landing craft. Jagged shell fragments killed and wounded a number of Marines.

The helmsman of one Higgins Boat was struck down at the wheel. The vessel, momentarily out of control, yawed about and headed back toward Gavutu.

Other helmsmen, confused by the accident, believed a withdrawal had been ordered and turned their craft to follow the first one. As a result, only three Higgins Boats went on to the beach where a torrent of lead from mortars and automatic weapons greeted them.

The Marines disembarked and ran along a bulkhead to regroup for the push inland. The light from the fires made the crouching Leathernecks easy targets for enemy gunners. Baker Company's casualties soared quickly and the CO, Captain Edgar Crane, radioed for boats to evacuate his men.

The offensive against both Gavutu and Tanambogo was resumed on Saturday, August 8, at daybreak. Blue Battalion, 2nd Marines, landed on Gavutu and by 1600 (4:00 P.M.) only isolated resistance was left. The battalion was then pulled out of the line. Some of its companies marched to Tanambogo across the causeway, while others came there by sea. Two light tanks supported the water-borne attack. They rattled ashore from the landing craft with machine guns spitting. As the tanks rolled along the beach, the Marines were given a sample of Japanese fanaticism.

A mob of about 50 Nipponese poured out of caves and

foxholes and hurled themselves upon the tanks. They scrambled up the sides and pounded on the hatches with rifle butts, iron bars, and rocks. One tank was put out of commission when a Japanese soldier, at the cost of his own life, rammed a crowbar between its treads. The crippled vehicle was then set afire by a barrage of Molotov cocktails. The crewmen scrambled out of the burning tank only to be killed by the Japanese.

By this time, the Marines who had landed behind the tanks began shooting into the milling crowd of enemy soldiers. As a Leatherneck rifleman remembered it ". . . the Japs were so busy trying to bust into the second tank, they never even noticed us picking them off one by one. It was like shooting clay pigeons."

Every Japanese around the tanks was killed. The fight for Tanambogo did not slacken until almost midnight when Marine signal rockets above Tulagi and Gavutu indicated those islands were secure. In the struggle for these harbor islands the Marines suffered total casualties of 15 officers and 233 enlisted men of whom eight officers and 100 enlisted men were killed. Enemy losses were far greater. About 1500 men had garrisoned Tulagi, Gavutu, and Tanambogo. Less than 100 survived.

Battle-weary U.S. Marines dug in on the newly conquered territory. As a heavy tropical rain began to fall, the focus of the struggle swung back to Guadalcanal, where it was to stay for many months.

CHAPTER THREE

Savo Island

AUGUST 9, 1942

Three

1

Vice Admiral Gunichi Mikawa, CO, 8th Fleet, Imperial Navy, with headquarters at Rabaul, New Britain, sat down to breakfast at 0700 (7:00 A.M.) Friday, August 7, 1942. Clad in a spotless, starched white uniform, Mikawa was a stern-faced, unsmiling man with a big jaw and a firm mouth.

Sipping his breakfast tea, the Admiral contemplated the bustling scene in Rabaul Harbor: battleships, cruisers, and destroyers of the 8th Fleet rode at anchor protected by barrage balloons and a vast concentration of AA guns. On adjacent airstrips, Zero (Zeke) fighters waited to repel any American plane that showed itself over Rabaul.

At the waterside, camouflaged warehouses were cram-packed with the tools of war: weapons, ammunition, fuel, artillery, rations, medicines—everything to keep a great army in the field. Lorries rumbled back and forth at the docks. A company of infantry came marching past, fixed bayonets glinting in the sun; and over all, Mikawa could see the Rising Sun flag fluttering lazily from the harbor flagstaff.

As he leaned back in his chair, Mikawa must have been pleased at the view. Rabaul was a symbol of Nippon's power in the Pacific. However, the admiral's prideful satisfaction was disturbed by a perspiring orderly who handed him a sealed blue envelope from Rabaul Message Center. The envelope's color indicated the despatch was urgent.

When Mikawa read the message, he flushed with dismay. Yankee Marines had landed on Guadalcanal and Tulagi under cover of naval and aerial bombardment! This news was both shocking and incredible. His leisurely breakfast forgotten, the admiral scurried back to his office. Soon, he had motorcycle couriers roaring off with orders instructing Rabaul army commanders to ready their men for immediate embarkation on the six transports moored in the anchorage. The troops were reinforcements for the garrisons on Guadalcanal and Tulagi.

Mikawa also commanded five heavy cruisers, on patrol duty off Rabaul, to return at once. He meant to assault the Americans with a strong naval surface force. Rabaul-based planes were sent to bomb American ships then landing supplies and men on Guadalcanal. The impudent Yankees would soon feel the weight of Japanese strength on land, sea, and air.

Two of Mikawa's counterthrusts failed. Coastwatchers forewarned the Americans; and the Japanese planes were shot out of the sky. The hastily assembled troop transports, escorted by destroyers, weighed anchor and began the long run down the Slot to Guadalcanal. They did not get far. The *S-38,* an obsolescent nineteen-year-old U.S. submarine, happened to be cruising in the area. She proved herself no candidate for the scrap pile by putting a spread of torpedoes into Mikawa's biggest transport, the 5,600 ton *Meiyo Maru,* which went down with 14 officers and 328 enlisted men aboard. Despite Japanese depth charges, the aged *S-38* made a nimble escape.

Mikawa recalled all his transports after the *Meiyo Maru* was sunk. He thought the Americans had a submarine cordon in the waters off Rabaul. The time was not right to reinforce Guadalcanal.

The admiral pinned everything on the third part of his plan, an attack by a swift and hard-hitting naval force.

This phase began at 1628 (4:28 P.M.) August 7, when Mikawa hauled his red and white striped flag to the foremast of the heavy cruiser *Chokai* which steamed out of Rabaul harbor followed by the light cruisers *Tenryu* and *Yubari* to rendezvous with four other heavies and one destroyer. When the forces joined, the flotilla raced for Guadalcanal.

The decision was made to attack during the pre-dawn hours of Sunday, August 9. "We liked the idea that our blow was to be made on a Sunday. It smacked of Pearl Harbor for us. Every man was determined to repeat the glorious achievements of that Sunday morning eight months before. No one doubted success. Our Navy was highly trained in night fighting, while the Americans were unskilled in this type of naval combat," a Japanese staff officer recorded in his journal.

Admiral Mikawa knew he was taking a long chance. The success of a night attack relied on surprise. He needed good luck to avoid detection by American search planes since his ships would be in the open all day August 8. The Admiral's luck was better than good—it was phenomenal.

His ships were spotted at 1026 (10:26 A.M.) Saturday, August 8, by an Australian Hudson patrol-bomber. At 1101 (11:01 A.M.) a second Aussie Hudson saw them. The planes trailed the Japanese until driven off by the cruisers' AA guns.

A string of blunders, plus poor judgment and inefficiency by his enemies then provided all the luck Mikawa needed. The pilots of the Hudsons should have realized that the presence of a strong enemy naval flotilla, only 350 miles from Guadalcanal, constituted a threat to the American landings.

For reasons still not known, the first flier, who had orders to break radio silence if a report was sufficiently urgent, did not do so. Instead, he finished his search patterns, returned to base at Milne Bay, had tea, and only then mentioned Mikawa's ships. Because of this negligence the crucial intelligence did not come to Admiral Turner's attention until 1845 (6:45 P.M.) August 8.

By then it was too late for Turner to do anything about the enemy force. U.S. planes could never locate the Japanese at night. Besides, foul weather had descended along the entire length of the Slot, giving Mikawa added concealment.

The Japanese admiral had not wasted the daylight hours

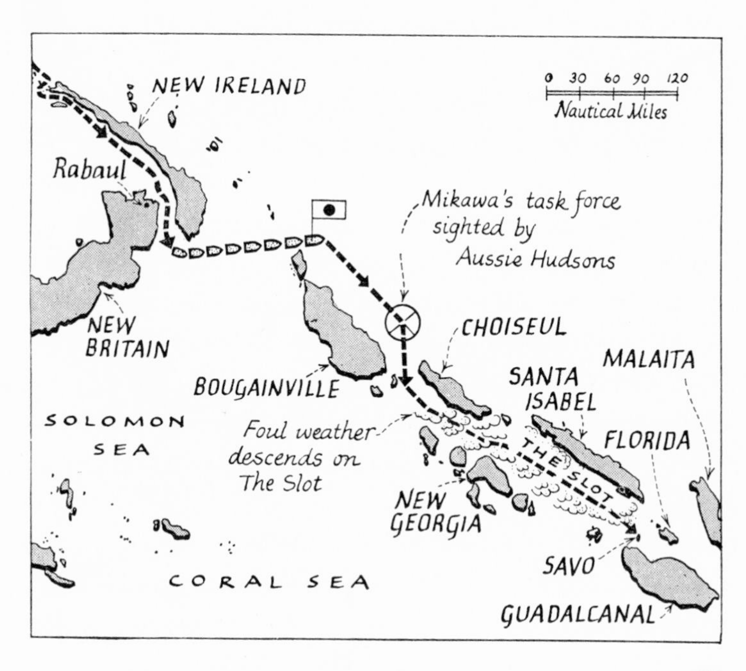

of August 8. He launched floatplanes from two cruisers. These aircraft reconnoitered the American ships off Guadalcanal and Tulagi, returning safely despite vigorous AA fire.

Mikawa's pilots listed many targets in the narrow waters of Sealark Channel between Guadalcanal and Tulagi: one battleship, six cruisers, 19 destroyers, and 18 transports.

This was all Mikawa needed to know. He continued down the Slot at 24 knots and ordered his sailors to prepare for battle. The admiral also drew up a plan which was passed on to every ship by blinker signal:

> "On the rush-in we will go from south of Savo Island and torpedo the enemy main force in front of the Guadalcanal anchorage; after which we will turn toward the Tulagi forward area to shell and torpedo the enemy. We will then withdraw north of Savo Island."

Having transmitted his battle plan, Mikawa sent more scout planes for a final daylight check of the American ships. The pilots reported the enemy fleet had not moved. At 1840 (6:40 P.M.) Mikawa sent a final message to his men:

"Let us attack with certain victory in the traditional night attack of the Imperial Navy! May each one calmly do his utmost!"

He then retired to his cabin for a rest. Perhaps, as he was

waiting for sleep to come, the admiral may have felt some doubts over the outcome of this operation. He must have felt uneasy for an aide noted: ". . . the admiral emerged from his cabin and went to the bridge where he remained all through the night . . . this was most unusual . . . I believe he stayed there because he did not want to be alone . . ."

2

Admiral Mikawa need have had no qualms about the outcome of his mission. Its success was assured when Admiral Frank Jack Fletcher advised Admiral Turner on August 8 that the U.S. aircraft carriers were being withdrawn after remaining only thirty-six hours in the combat zone.

According to Fletcher he could not linger because his fighter strength had been cut from 99 Wildcats to 78. He was also worried over reports that Japanese torpedo planes and dive-bombers were present in considerable numbers. Most important (Fletcher said) was the critical fuel shortage of his destroyers and cruisers.

For these reasons he recommended ". . . the immediate withdrawal of my carriers."

Turner argued with him by radio. He broke down each of Fletcher's reasons. Even with only 78 Wildcats, the Americans had one more fighter plane than had been available at Midway. The destroyers and cruisers could be refueled from fleet oilers at their positions off San Cristobal Island, 120 miles southeast of Savo. Turner pointed out the danger to the transport fleet and the invasion forces if Fletcher took away the carriers. At the least, he urged, let the carriers cover the operation for the promised 72 hours.

Fletcher remained adamant. He seemed convinced that his carriers and their escorts were in imminent peril of an overwhelming Japanese attack. A colleague of his later wrote, ". . . I believe that Admiral Fletcher temporarily lost his nerve at Guadalcanal . . . perhaps he was haunted by the losses of the *Lexington* and the *Yorktown* . . . no man can say what went through his mind . . . obviously, he was fearful of suffering loss or damage to the *Wasp, Enterprise,* or *Saratoga* . . . and ordered the ships to move southward even before Comsopac granted permission to pull out. . . ."

No matter what prompted Fletcher's hasty departure, the fact was that he had left the naval vessels and transports off Guadalcanal without air cover. And as the carriers steamed away, Turner heard of a new peril. At 1845 (6:45 P.M.) he was handed the report that a big Japanese surface force was heading his way—Mikawa and his cruisers.

This news did nothing to improve Turner's feelings. But he prepared to meet the situation and signaled Admiral Crutchley to deploy the destroyers and cruiser screen at predetermined battle stations.

In order to protect the transports off Guadalcanal and Tulagi, the waters between Florida, Savo, and Guadalcanal (soon to be known as Ironbottom Sound because of the many ships that were sunk there) had been divided into four defensive sectors.

The guard force under Crutchley's command consisted of the cruisers *Australia, Canberra* (both Australian), and *Chicago.* In the Northern Force Captain Frederick Riefkohl commanded the *Quincy,* the *Vincennes,* and the *Astoria* (all U.S. Navy), plus two American destroyers.

The *Blue* and the *Ralph Talbot,* radar-equipped "tin cans," took up their picket duty off the western tip of Savo Island. The eastern approaches to Guadalcanal were watched by two light cruisers, the American *San Juan* and the Australian *Hobart,* along with U.S. destroyers *Monssen* and *Buchanan.* These ships were commanded by Rear Admiral Norman Scott, USN.

The sentry units began patrolling. To the south: the *Australia,* the *Canberra,* and the *Chicago;* to the north between Florida and Savo, the *Vincennes,* the *Quincy,* and the *Astoria.*

When he had been notified that the guard ships were posted, Turner signaled both Crutchley and General Vandegrift at 2032 (8:32 P.M.) to attend a command conference aboard the *McCawley.*

Vandegrift was at the 1st Marine Division CP reviewing the day's events with his staff when Turner's message arrived. The general was satisfied with the way things had gone on the invasion beaches. His men had performed well. Only one sore spot troubled him—the unloading of the supply ships lagged badly. At Tulagi, few vessels had even started to put cargo ashore, while almost half the division's equipment was still aboard the ships off Guadalcanal.

Unloading had stopped for the night when the transports hauled anchor and made for the open sea. Turner considered it too risky for them in the narrow waters of Sealark Channel where Japanese bombers could get at them. The cargo ships were to return next morning and resume unloading, this time at a better pace, it was hoped.

Turner's unexpected message did not make Vandegrift feel that anything was amiss. He surmised that the admiral wanted a first hand report on the situation ashore.

In a cheerful mood, General Vandegrift called for his launch and set out to the *McCawley* anchored in midchannel off Lunga Point. From his battle station 20 miles away, Admiral Crutchley also responded to Turner's summons. The Royal Navy officer hurried to the meeting aboard his flagship, the cruiser *Australia*. He came by ship because a motor boat would have taken several hours for the trip. When the *Australia* was withdrawn from picket duty, a gap opened in the ranks of the southern defensive group.

Crutchley and Vandegrift were aboard the *McCawley*

by 2330 (11:30 P.M.). Admiral Turner greeted them curtly and blurted out Fletcher's removal of the aircraft carriers. As if this was not bad news enough, Turner gave them some more. Due to the lack of air cover, he had decided the transports, although only partially unloaded, must leave before daybreak.

Vandegrift was dismayed. His Marines, now 18,000, were going to be abandoned in hostile territory with insufficient food and ammunition. Yet he saw Turner had no alternative. All that shipping could not be left to the mercy of Japanese planes which would now have complete aerial supremacy.

The Marine general did manage to convince Turner that the transports should be called back for an all-night unloading operation. The most needed material would be put ashore at Tulagi and Guadalcanal. Although Turner stilled feared a night air raid, he agreed to take his chances so that the Marines could have a stockpile to supply their immediate needs. The admiral also mentioned reports of an enemy surface force coming down the Slot at that very moment.

"I'm not worried about those ships," Turner said. "We've made proper provisions to deal with such an attack. No enemy vessel will get through our guard cordon."

The conference ended shortly before midnight. Crutchley returned to the *Australia;* Vandegrift went to Tulagi for a meeting with his second-in-command, Brigadier General

William Rupertus, to appraise him of the unpleasant new developments.

Out in the dark waters of Ironbottom Sound, the U.S. patrols moved slowly on their rounds. The night was hot, humid, and quiet. Off Savo Island, a sudden squall blew up and visibility was curtailed. Lookouts, straining to pierce the gloom, could barely see anything a hundred yards away. On board the U.S. and Australian cruisers and picketing destroyers men paced the decks, searching the stillness through night glasses.

Overhead came the drone of airplane motors, but since the craft had running lights on, lookouts assumed them to be friendly. No hostile airman would court death by flying above an enemy fleet with lights on, an easy target for AA gunners. Those planes were American, everyone who saw them decided.

3

For reasons still unexplained, no effort was taken to check the identity of the aircraft. The destroyer *Ralph Talbot* had spotted the planes on her radar screen and sent an alarm by radio: "Warning—Warning: plane over Savo headed east!"

The destroyer's communications officer had done his duty. It was not his fault that a sudden electrical storm garbled the message so badly that it was unintelligible aboard the *McCawley,* cruising only twenty miles away.

Other American and Australian ships heard the planes, picked them up on radar or made visual observations. Nobody fired at them, since no orders to shoot had come from Turner. It was standard operating procedure that no vessel was to open fire unless the command was given by Admiral Turner.

As a result, everyone thought the admiral knew all about the planes, when actually he had no knowledge of them at all.

The two planes had been launched by one of Mikawa's cruisers at 2313 (11:13 P.M.). The pilots had orders to remain over the American fleet and be in position to release flares when the attacking cruisers arrived.

Admiral Mikawa was incredibly optimistic even to harbor the hope that his pilots could get away with such a stunt. However, his arrogance bred contempt for the Americans. Mikawa was certain the plan would succeed because he had willed it.

The admiral was determined to strike the Americans a crushing blow even if it cost every ship he commanded and took the lives of all the men aboard them—including his own. The task force steamed ahead, sparked by this spirit.

On the bridge of the *Chokai,* Admiral Mikawa checked the reports coming from his scout planes. Once, he permitted himself a flickering smile when word arrived that the transports, which had moved out of the channel, were at that very moment returning to their daytime moorings.

"The sheep had returned to the fold," a *Chokai* officer jotted in his diary. "We were the wolves about to fall on them . . ."

The Japanese cruisers went on without incident or interruption. Nothing challenged Mikawa's advance. The crews of his ships were ready for action. Shells and torpedoes had been racked up in the magazines; fuzed, primed, and ready for firing. The sailors were relaxed; they laughed, joked, and sang songs. From his place on the bridge, Admiral Mikawa nodded approval at the high morale of the men on his flagship.

Mikawa studied the other ships following the *Chokai* in fighting array: the heavy cruisers *Aoba, Kako, Kinugasa* and *Furutaka;* the light cruisers *Tenryu* and *Yubari* brought up the rear while the destroyer *Yunagi* ran along the column's flank.

Admiral Mikawa was pleased. Although this was a hastily assembled force and none of the ships had ever seen action as a unit before, he knew officers and men would not fail him.

At 0045 (12:45 A.M.) the Mikawa Task Force entered the head of Ironbottom Sound and the *Chokai's* signalman blinkered "Battle Stations Alerted!" to the trailing ships. Now that they were in enemy territory, Mikawa quickly reviewed his plan: to hit the ships off Guadalcanal, cross Sealark Channel and get those at Tulagi, then make a quick getaway to be beyond carrier plane range by daylight.

A fine scheme—if it worked; if the Americans were taken off guard. Perhaps, even Mikawa felt a twinge of worry at that moment. He was in enemy dominated waters and any second might bring the roar of Yankee guns or the shattering crash of torpedoes as the Japanese ships were discovered.

But his incredible luck held out. The squadron rode past the U.S. destroyer *Blue* at a distance of 4,000 yards. Every Japanese gun was trained upon the *Blue* ready to blast her out of the water should the "tin can" give any sign of having seen Mikawa's ships. But the *Blue's* lookouts must have been searching elsewhere and her radar sweeping other areas, for Task Force Mikawa slipped by without raising any alarm.

At 0136 (1:36 A.M.) the Japanese reached Savo Island. The marauders were almost in position. Visual sightings were made of American destroyers and cruisers. Mikawa nodded brusquely to his signal officer. "Tell them to pick targets and commence the action!" he snapped.

Moments later torpedo tubes were being angled and guns sighted. It was 0143 (1:43 A.M.) when the U.S. destroyer *Patterson* spotted the Japanese at a range of 5,000 yards. They broadcast a radio alarm. An emergency signal was flashed to all the guard force: "Warning—Warning: strange ships entering harbor!"

But even as the frantic message was crackling over the air waves, the Americans were too late. The circling scout planes dropped calcium flares to illuminate the American ships with a weird, greenish light. Japanese torpedoes hissed and splashed toward their victims.

The *Chokai, Aoba,* and *Furutaka* loosed one salvo after another. Torpedoes smashed into the Australian cruiser *Canberra* and that ship was torn by awful explosions as her General Quarters alarm sounded.

The *Chicago* sagged helplessly, bracketed by shells, her bow blown off by a "tin fish." The *Patterson* took a beating but fought back gallantly with her four-inch guns and even launched a few torpedoes which missed the target.

The U.S. Naval forces were swept by confusion. Ships hastily cleared for action and some American guns fired at the onrushing foe. But Mikawa had them by the throat.

Mikawa turned his attack on the northern group. The *Chokai* fired and the U.S.S. *Astoria* went up in flames.

"She burned like a funeral pyre," an eye witness recorded.

The *Quincy* scored a timely hit on the *Chokai,* smashing her chart room and killing a number of officers and men. However, seconds after, the *Quincy* was caught in the searchlight beams of three Nipponese ships and pounded to pieces. The *Vincennes* struck the *Kinugasa,* causing some damage, but she also received mortal wounds and went down.

The crashing reverberations of the big guns startled the Marines ashore. Someone raised the cry that Japanese troops were landing at Lunga Point and a hurricane of lead churned the beach. The sounds of the naval clash interrupted General Vandegrift's meeting with General Rupertus on Tulagi.

The two officers stared at each other in stunned silence.

THE BATTLE OF THE FIVE SITTING DUCKS

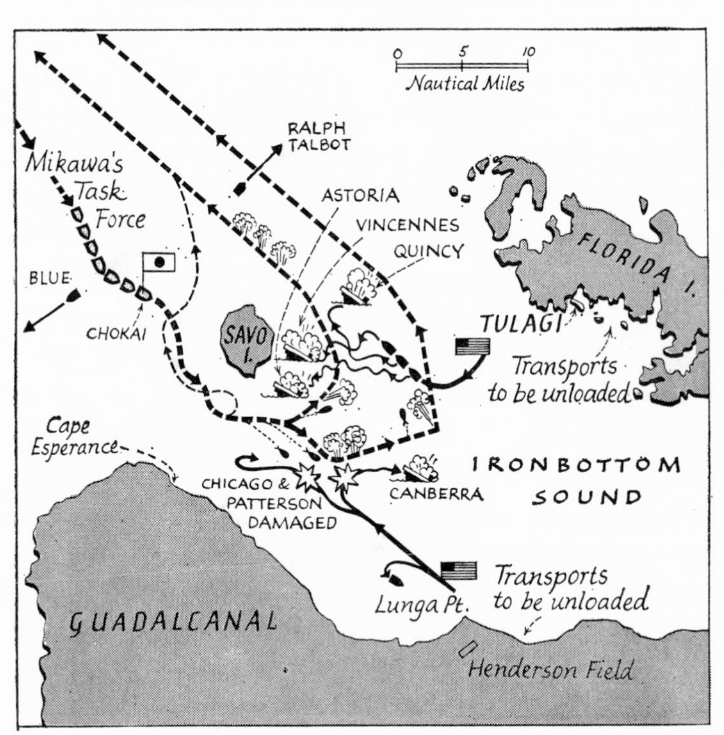

Both realized the shooting and the explosions could only mean that the Japanese surface fleet had broken through the cordon.

Aboard the transports, sailors worked desperately to haul anchor and get up steam, but the skippers were afraid to move. No one knew where the enemy would next appear. So the Americans listened and waited in mounting apprehension as the battle's fury rose to a crescendo.

The dark waters of Ironbottom Sound were dotted with the hulks of burning ships; there was no longer need for flares to light the scene as Mikawa continued his deadly work; the flames gave off enough illumination.

The admiral's heart was high. His force was almost intact, only the *Chokai* and the *Kinugasa* had been damaged and American shell splinters had caused some casualties on the *Aoba*. Seldom had an officer of the Imperial Navy won such a complete success so swiftly.

However, Mikawa's battle formation had become disarranged in the melee. His ships were so dispersed that he had difficulty keeping in touch with them. Fearful of being caught at daybreak by American carrier planes, Mikawa ordered a retreat without going after the transports which had been his main target. Had he known of Fletcher's withdrawal, Mikawa could have massacred the cargo ships. Instead, at 0240 (2:40 A.M.), the Japanese fleet had pulled out of the Sound and was dashing up the Slot at a swift 30 knots.

On the way home, Mikawa checked his losses: they were slim indeed, superficial damages to three ships and casualties totaling 58 killed and 53 wounded. Small wonder that his sailors chanted victory songs and toasted the Mikado in *sake* that was doled out to all hands. It had been a glorious triumph for the Sons of Nippon.

"Our joy was unbounded," an officer on the *Chokai* noted in his diary. "The Imperial Navy was supreme!"

If the Japanese were happy, the Americans faced Sunday, August 9, with gloom. The quickly won victories on Guadalcanal and Tulagi, Gavutu, and Tanambogo, had suddenly gone sour. Four cruisers were sunk, a fifth fearfully battered, and two destroyers sunk.

Naval historians called that action of August 8–9 the Battle of Savo Island; but the U.S. sailors and Marines, more accurately dubbed it the Battle of the Five Sitting Ducks, referring to the cruisers that had been destroyed by the enemy.

Still, everything was not all black. Admiral Turner announced that the transports would remain for unloading. Men worked feverishly to get supplies off, momentarily expecting another Japanese surface attack or big air raids. However, for unknown reasons, the enemy did not interfere. By late afternoon, August 9, the transports sailed for Nouméa, emptied of their cargo.

The Marines were alone on Guadalcanal and the other islands with only light naval forces to guard their seaward flank. The U.S. Navy had been badly mauled in its first surface action since the Battle of Santiago during the Spanish-American War. The casualties of the disaster off Savo Island were high—1,023 killed, 709 wounded and most of the American and Australian cruiser strength sent to the mud of Ironbottom Sound.

American spirits lifted somewhat on August 10, with the news that the U.S. submarine, *S-44,* had exacted some vengeance for Savo Island by torpedoing the cruiser *Kako* off Rabaul. She went under in five minutes with few survivors, while the *S-44* got away scot free.

This counterblow blunted the Japanese triumph and served to awaken the belief that the struggle for Guadalcanal was going to be cruel, long, and costly to both sides.

CHAPTER FOUR

Tenaru River

AUGUST 21, 1942

Four

1

There were hard times on Guadalcanal after the Battle of Savo Island. The 1st Marine Division, in Leatherneck slang, had to "sweat it out." No big-gunned warships protected them from the Imperial Navy which now had free run of the surrounding waters. The Marines had no planes to guard against bombing and strafing attacks.

"Nobody was giving odds on our chances," a staff officer admitted.

Food was a major problem. From the very outset, it had to be rationed. Since slow moving transports were more liable to attack by planes, surface craft, or subs, provisions were brought in at infrequent intervals on swift destroyers which dashed down from Nouméa when possible.

The men on Guadalcanal were always hungry. "We used to spend hours talking about food—rare steaks smothered in onions and mushrooms, juicy roast beef, dumplings, apple pie, ice cream—stuff like that. And when Marines talk food instead of girls, you *know* they're hungry!" a sergeant said.

But from General Vandegrift to the rear-rank privates, all hands pretended cheerfulness. Men reassured one another that reinforcements would soon be on the way. "Don't worry, Mac! Uncle Sam won't let us down! The Navy'll come back!"

Despite all their optimism, the Marines knew what could happen. The disasters on Bataan and Corregidor in the Philippines were still fresh. The Bataan "Death March" had taken place only a few months earlier. The immediate future seemed bleak to the Marines.

Though trained for attack, they assumed the defensive on Guadalcanal—which everybody quickly called The Canal. The mass opinion was that the Japs were going to have a tough job retaking the island—and no one doubted they would soon attempt to do so.

General Vandegrift drew up a plan of defense. His Marines were to complete the airfield, haul the supplies off the beach, and dig in to prevent any large scale enemy counter-landings.

The main defense lines set up along the Tenaru River in the east, described an arc to Kukum Village on the Lunga River to the west. Patrols constantly probed the jungle trails in all directions looking for the Japanese who had garrisoned on Guadalcanal.

Starting on Sunday, August 9, Japanese planes began to bomb the Marine positions. The only weapons the Leathernecks had to fight off these attacks were unwieldy 90-mm AA guns. "We might as well have tried throwing rocks at the Nips," a Marine said. "The bombers gave us a real tough time."

But neither bombs nor adversity could crush Marine morale. The men worked long hours to complete Henderson Field. It was hard work, done without proper tools or equipment. The daily rains turned the dirt runway into a quagmire so deep that trucks and jeeps sank to their headlights in mud. But after the rains, the sun baked the ground to the hardness of concrete.

As a result of this Marine labor, a Catalina (PBY) patrol-bomber made a trial landing. General Vandegrift signaled Admiral Ghormley on Thursday, August 17, that the field was operable in dry weather. Vandegrift was told he could expect a flight of Dauntless (SBD) bombers soon.

Supply destroyers rushed in with aviation gas, bombs, and airplane spare parts, and the Marines eagerly awaited the planes. However, before they arrived, trouble again hounded the Leathernecks.

One of Vandegrift's problems was to learn precisely where the survivors of the enemy garrison had holed up. The strong resistance his patrols met near the Matanikau River suggested the Japanese main force lay there.

This was confirmed when a talkative Japanese naval warrant officer was captured. He admitted that most of his countrymen still on Guadalcanal were dug in across the Matanikau and also expressed the belief they were ready to surrender. Later, a Marine patrol sighted a white flag displayed near the Matanikau. This convinced Lt. Col. Frank B. Goettge (D-2) that: ". . . the Japs are sick and starving and could easily be made prisoner . . ."

Goettge organized a lightly armed 25-man patrol, carrying rations and medicines, to make a reconnaissance by launch, and land on the beach west of the Matanikau River, near where the "surrender" flag had been seen.

On Wednesday, August 12, just before daybreak, Goettge's party went ashore near the enemy position. Instead of finding a meekly surrendering enemy, the Americans blundered into a machine gun ambush. All but three men were killed.

Angry Marines swore to avenge their comrades. They vowed to kill every Japanese who fell into their hands. "Remember Goettge!" became a war cry on The Canal.

At the time, the Americans could not have known that the Japanese at the Matanikau never intended to surrender. The white flag they flew was no sign of capitulation but an Imperial battle flag hanging limply from its staff so the folds hid the red Rising Sun insignia. The garrulous prisoner had meant no treachery. He had only expressed an honest opinion about the feelings of his fellow Japanese.

The Americans took some revenge for Goettge on August 19 when three companies of the 5th Marines, supported by field artillery, raided enemy positions at the Matanikau. After a brief but spirited fight, in which the Marines killed 65 Japanese while losing four men, the Leathernecks entered both Kokumbona and Matanikau villages, blew up some enemy installations, and then fell back across the Matanikau.

This was only the first installment exacted for the Goettge patrol. The Marines were soon to collect a more sizable payment on the eastern flank of their defensive zone, the Tenaru River, as a result of high-level decisions made in Tokyo and Rabaul.

THE GOETTGE PATROL MEETS DISASTER

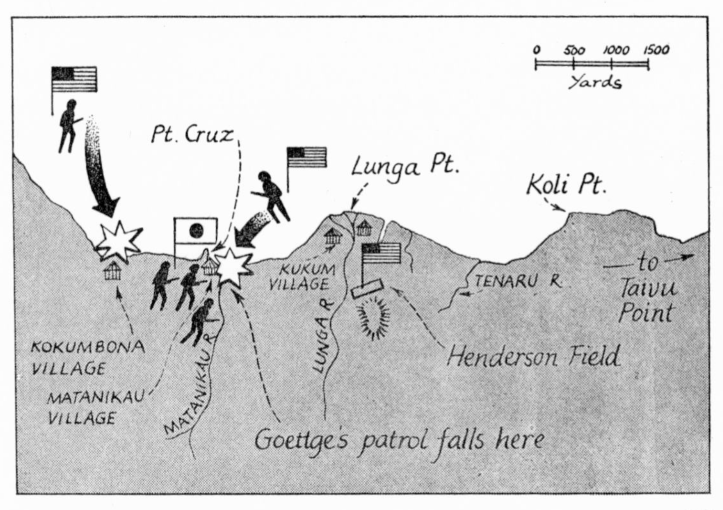

2

At the express wish of the Emperor, Premier Hideki Tojo, head of the Japanese government, issued orders that the Americans must be driven out of Guadalcanal and the adjacent islands. The Emperor willed it.

To lead the work of "annihilating the Americans," Tojo chose Lt. General Harukichi Hyakutate, CO, Imperial 17th Army. The Premier flew to Hyakutate's headquarters at Rabaul and personally gave him the assignment.

The general, a skinny dyspeptic man, hid his displeasure. Up to that time he had been preparing a plan for capturing the Allied base of Port Moresby, New Guinea, the gateway to Australia.

Visions of glory dazzled the general. The man who took Port Moresby would be forever enshrined in Japanese history. With this dream in mind, Hyakutate toiled hours perfecting his plans. In his heart, the general knew it could not fail. Now, this grand opportunity was taken from him because the Yankees had landed Marines on Guadalcanal and its neighboring islands.

General Hyakutate was chagrined at his new position; he considered it a downgrading. Guadalcanal meant nothing to him. It was merely a foul outpost of little significance in the Pacific War. But, as a soldier, the general had no alternative except to obey his orders.

Through a colossal blunder, Japanese Intelligence estimated the number of Marines on Guadalcanal at only 2,000 men and another 2,000 on Tulagi, Gavutu, and Tanambogo. The count was ludicrously wrong. There were at the time (August 12) 10,000 Marines on Guadalcanal and approximately 3,000 on the other islands.

Guided by this erroneous report, General Hyakutate decided he needed less than a single battalion (1,500 men) to do the job. The general had little regard for the fighting qualities of American troops.

He picked an elite battalion, the Ichiki Detachment, named for its CO, Colonel Kiyonao Ichiki, as the unit to crush the Guadalcanal Marines. The Ichikis, stationed at Guam, boarded transports there for the run to the Japanese Naval Base at Truk, where Colonel Ichiki and 916 of his men embarked on six destroyers and sped down the Slot to Guadalcanal.

In its early stages the Japanese counterlanding went off without a hitch. The destroyers slipped undetected past the American positions on the night of August 18 and put the 900 Ichikis ashore. At daybreak, August 19, the six destroyers were in Sealark Channel bombarding the Marines on Tulagi and at Lunga Point. Shells tore up the Henderson Field runway and wrought damage on Tulagi, but the destroyers had to dash for safety when U.S. Army Flying Fortresses (B-17) droned in from the American air base on Espiritu Santo and unloaded tons of bombs all around the Imperial Navy ships.

It was not easy for a B-17 to hit a zigzagging destroyer from 20,000 feet. The Forts rarely scored on moving targets. But that morning a B-17 bombardier dropped a 500-pound "egg" dead center on the destroyer *Hazikaze* which limped away trailing smoke, her forward turrets twisted into a formless mass.

3

The Americans attached no special significance to the naval bombardment and knew few details of the Point Taivu landings. Marine patrols did not venture that far from the Tenaru River. However, during the afternoon of August 19, an unusual incident occurred in the jungle between Point Taivu and the Tenaru River.

A Marine patrol led by Captain Charles Brush ambushed a 34-man party of Japanese who were out laying wire. Of the enemy, 31 were killed outright. The survivors fled into the bush and disappeared. The Marines might have written off the episode as an unimportant jungle clash except that orders found on one of the dead officers made Captain Brush realize that the men were from a newly arrived unit which was coming to attack the Marines on the Tenaru.

Captain Brush brought this intelligence to Lieutenant Colonel Edwin Pollock, CO, White Battalion, 1st Marines, who commanded the position. Pollock deployed his men for the attack, figuring it would be aimed at a sandspit that bridged the sluggish river.

The Leathernecks rigged booby traps along the barbed wire apron they had erected. Col. Pollock also fortified a coconut grove on the opposite bank of the river; a good place from which to enfilade the attackers. He scattered outposts through the jungle and along the trails. A battery of 37-mm cannon was wheeled into position. The Marines were ready.

They waited all night, but no enemy came. However, Pollock did not lower his guard. He strengthened his positions and kept patrols moving out in front.

As the Marines on the Tenaru prepared for an enemy assault, good news came to Guadalcanal. Just after sunrise, August 20, the auxiliary aircraft carrier *Long Island* arrived off San Cristobal Island where she turned into the wind and catapulted 19 Wildcats and 12 Dauntlesses manned by Marine pilots. The fliers circled the ship once and then followed their leader, Lieutenant Colonel Charles L. Fike, on a beeline for Henderson Field.

The Wildcats and Dauntlesses came over Guadalcanal at tree-top height and the Marines, fearing an air raid, dived into slit trenches, and bomb shelters. Then someone spied the white stars painted on the wings of the aircraft and let out a happy yell. Men ran into the open, shouting, waving, turning somersaults, pounding each other on the back, and crying for joy as the planes buzzed up and down the

Marine-held sectors so that every Leatherneck on Guadalcanal would know help had come.

Fike's air group made bumpy landings on the shell-torn field and stared in dismay at the crude facilities. However, the lack of a good airstrip did not keep them from taking the air, August 21, and shooting down a Zero (Zeke) fighter. The fliers also played a part in the battle that was shaping up to the east as Colonel Ichiki led his men from Point Taivu to the Tenaru River.

Word that the enemy was at hand came to Colonel Pollock from his patrols and outposts. The Japanese were pushing through the jungle in considerable numbers. At 0130, August 21, a calcium flare rose out of the jungle. A knot of yowling, bayonet-wielding Ichikis, led by officers waving *samurai* swords, burst from amid the foliage and rushed out onto the sandspit.

The enemy hurled hand grenades, fired rifles and screamed "*Banzai!*" The attackers halted briefly at the barbed wire. Booby traps went off; wounded Japanese shrieked and the Marines opened up with rifles, machine guns, mortars, and the 37-mm cannon. But not even this deadly fire could turn back the Nipponese.

Many reached the American lines and Marines leaped out of foxholes to grapple with them hand-to-hand. Grenades popped, pistols cracked; men wrestled in the river muck, slashing with knives and bayonets. It was a wild, ferocious struggle.

The fight raged until daybreak (August 21) when the Japanese, stumbling over their dead comrades, fled across the sandspit.

"Go get 'em!" Colonel Pollock roared. The Marines surged after the beaten foe.

Some Ichiki survivors ran to the beach and plunged into the sea where Marine rifle bullets killed them. Others made for the coconut grove in which Pollock had placed his men. The Japanese were met with machine gun fire from the grove. A few managed to dig in amid the coconut trees. They resisted until Marine tanks crashed into the

THE ICHIKI DETACHMENT WIPED OUT

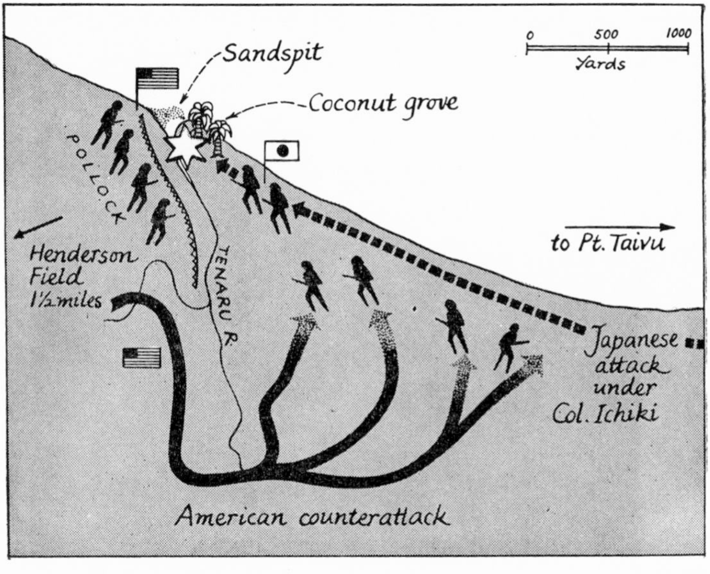

grove followed by Red Battalion, 1st Marines. The fragments of Colonel Ichiki's elite detachment were wiped out in a day long battle.

By sunset, August 21, it was all over. Nearly 1,000 Japanese soldiers had been killed in the attack. Because they fought from entrenched positions, the Marines lost only 35 dead and 75 wounded. The low American casualty rate was also due to the fighting skill of the Marines.

Among the Japanese dead was Colonel Ichiki. Just before the battle ended, he burned the detachment's colors and shot himself through the head. The survivors of his command fled into the jungle. Some perished there, others eventually linked up with other Japanese forces.

The myth that the Imperial Army was invincible died on the muddy banks of the Tenaru River that night. In their first meeting with U.S. Marines on nearly equal terms, the Mikado's soldiers showed themselves to be ordinary humans, who bled and died like anyone else, and could be beaten by brave men.

CHAPTER FIVE

Bloody Ridge

SEPTEMBER 14, 1942

Five

1

The news of what happened to the Ichiki Detachment filtered back to Rabaul. General Hyakutate received it with varying reactions. First he was skeptical, then outraged, and finally very worried. The Imperial General Staff in Tokyo was not going to be pleased. Incurring the displeasure of the Imperial Staff was no way for an ambitious general to advance his career.

Hyakutate might have been able to explain away the defeat if the Staff had not made the recapture of Guadalcanal a project of prime importance. Tojo called it "the first order of business."

Now General Hyakutate had to report on the results of the Ichiki Detachment mission. It was possible that he could cover up the catastrophic results by carefully phrasing his report. Hyakutate was renowned throughout the Imperial Army as an "artful dodger"—a man who had the talent to evade the truth of an unpleasant situation. He showed his skill along those lines in his official account to the Imperial Staff. "The attack . . . led by Colonel Ichiki was not entirely successful . . . but important results were attained . . ."

Hyakutate's deception did not fool the generals and admirals of the Imperial Staff. They understood what had happened to the Ichiki Detachment and wanted revenge. Orders were flashed to the general: "You will retake Guadalcanal before August is over."

This time, not only troops, but also a powerful naval force would participate in the counteroffensive. Admiral Isoruku Yamamoto, still smarting from his defeat at Midway, gathered a fleet of three aircraft carriers, three battleships, five cruisers, eight destroyers, and numerous auxiliary ships at the Truk Naval Base.

Simultaneously, Vice Admiral Nishizo Tsukahara mobilized four cruisers and five destroyers plus 100 airplanes at Rabaul. They were to participate in "Operation KA," the code name given to the recapture of Guadalcanal.

All the ships and planes had been gathered to support the landing of fresh troops near Point Taivu in approximately the same area where the ill-fated Ichiki Detachment had come ashore. By then, Hyakutate had received a revised estimate of Marine strength on Guadalcanal and now knew there were 13,000 and not 2,000 Marines holding it.

However, not even the disaster to the Ichikis altered his low regard of the Americans. "Colonel Ichiki had bad luck," was the way he wrote off the Marine victory.

The general decided that 1,500 well-equipped Japanese soldiers would be able to defeat the Americans. He mobilized survivors of the Ichiki Detachment (some 150 men who had not made the one-way trip to Guadalcanal) and attached them to a first-class brigade commanded by Major General Kiyotake Kawaguchi.

Meanwhile, as the troops were being assembled at Rabaul, and Admiral Yamamoto was gathering his naval units for the "big push," the Marines on The Canal were subjected to nightly bombardments by destroyers which came through the Slot to hit the Lunga Point positions. The Americans dubbed these nocturnal visitors the "Tokyo Express."

General Hyakutate decided to use the "Tokyo Express" for transporting the Kawaguchi Brigade to Point Taivu with the aid of aircraft and ships of the Combined Fleet. The planes would blast Henderson Field and destroy any American aerial opposition. Units of the Imperial Navy were to attack Yankee warships.

Operation KA began on Monday, August 24. The Combined Fleet steamed out to sea as the Kawaguchi Brigade marched up the gangplanks of the "Tokyo Express" destroyers at Rabaul. However, the Japanese preparations attracted the attention of U.S. reconnaissance planes and the word went out that the enemy was up to something big.

Comsopac started taking countermeasures. Admiral Fletcher was ordered to bring his carrier task forces back into the combat zone from Nouméa where they had been anchored since their hasty retreat from Guadalcanal on August 9.

Additional U.S. Naval strength was rushed to the Solomons. The carrier *Hornet* (with escorts) left Pearl Harbor on August 17. The battleships *Washington* and *South Dakota,* plus the AA cruiser *Juneau,* sailed through the Panama Canal for the South Pacific.

Planes from Fletcher's carriers found Yamamoto's main force on August 24. Japanese search planes located the U.S. fleet and a great naval air battle got underway. It lasted all day, August 24, and was continued after daylight, August 25, when the Japanese withdrew. The battle losses gave the Americans a slight edge. The big U.S. carrier *Enterprise* suffered heavy damage but was able to make it back to Nouméa for repairs. The Japanese lost the flattop *Ryujo* and so many planes that Admiral Nobutake Kondo, commanding the Combined Fleet Air Arm, had to draw back his ships.

As the flattops were slugging it out at sea, planes defending Henderson Field downed about 5 bombers and 17 Zekes. On August 25, the day the naval engagement ended, a Marine scout plane spotted Japanese troop-carrying transports steaming through the Slot. Marine fliers went up after the enemy.

At 0935 (9:35 A.M.) a Dauntless dive bomber piloted by Marine Second Lieutenant Lawrence Baldinus reached the enemy convoy. He dropped a 1,000 pound bomb on the escorting cruiser *Jintsu,* the flagship, which carried Rear Admiral Raizu Tanaka. The projectile killed or wounded 61 men and set the cruiser afire.

Almost at the same moment, another SBD registered on the 9,300 ton transport *Kinryu Maru,* loaded with men of the Kawaguchi Brigade. The transport burst into flames and stopped dead. Although casualties were high, Admiral Tanaka still showed fight. Transferring his flag to a destroyer, he signalled the convoy to proceed after sending the *Jintsu* back to Truk under escort.

But the U.S. planes were not yet finished. Eight B-17's from Espiritu Santo attacked Tanaka's ship, sunk one destroyer and damaged another. This onslaught caused Tanaka to call off the daylight run to Guadalcanal. He ordered his remaining ships to the Japanese-held Shortland Islands near New Georgia. The troops debarked there to be picked up a few nights later by "Tokyo Express" destroyers and landed at Point Taivu under cover of darkness.

Although Fletcher's aircraft carriers and the Henderson Field planes had temporarily stalled General Hyakutate, life was made no easier for the Guadalcanal Marines.

Every night the "Tokyo Express" put troops ashore at Taivu until there were 1,500 men concentrated there under General Kawaguchi. Lunga Point was pounded by Japanese destroyers each night. While these bombardments caused little damage they kept the Marines from getting any rest.

The enemy added a new daily nuisance at chow time. As the Marines lined up for mess, a small Japanese patrol bomber arrived to drop anti-personnel missiles, causing the hungry Leathernecks to scramble for shelter.

This plane's engine had such a distinctive beat that the Marines called it "Washing-Machine Charlie." A few hours later, at bed time, a second small plane known as "Louie the Louse" showed up to loose another shower of fragmentation bombs.

"Louie the Louse" also accompanied the "Tokyo Express" destroyers and sent out calcium flares to light up the area for the enemy gunners. Both planes had incredible luck as Marine AA batteries wasted thousands of shells in unsuccessful efforts to bring them down.

During August, Henderson Field pilots fought many battles over Guadalcanal. They took a heavy toll of Zekes, Vals, Kates and Bettys. In less than a week, the scratch U.S. air force shot down 100 enemy aircraft at a cost of only 14 aircraft.

Cargo ships came to Lunga Point with rations and ammunition. Admiral Ghormley (Comsopac) set up submarine and surface patrols to guard against the numerically superior Imperial Navy. All planes that could be spared were rushed to Henderson Field. But if the Americans on The Canal received supplies, so did the Japanese.

With the regularity of a well-run railroad, the "Tokyo Express" brought men and supplies to Point Taivu and the Americans failed in their many attempts to derail it.

It was clear to the Marines on The Canal that the enemy was building up for an offensive. Early in September, Vandegrift prepared to meet this menace by bringing Edson's Raiders and the 1st Paramarines to Guadalcanal from Tulagi, Gavutu, and Tanambogo. The move was completed just in time. General Kawaguchi had ordered his men into the jungle to attack Henderson Field from the rear.

2

On paper, the plan Major General Kiyotake Kawaguchi had concocted to wipe out the U.S. Marines seemed perfect. It had several parts: the first was to capture Henderson Field; after that separate assaults would be simultaneously launched on both flanks; and last, an amphibious onslaught, supported by the carriers, battleships, cruisers, and destroyers of the Combined Fleet, would be hurled at the U.S. Lunga Point beachhead.

D-Day, Kawaguchi announced, was to be September 12. The enemy (he predicted) would be eliminated by October

10. He wrote his superior, General Hyakutate: ". . . by early October, Excellency, you will be able to move your operational headquarters from Rabaul to the airfield the Americans call Henderson Field . . . I give you my sacred pledge on this . . ."

Kawaguchi sent pioneer units to hack a trail in the jungle from Taivu to a spot southeast of Henderson Field where his infantry would jumpoff on D-Day. American reconnaissance planes spotted the trail makers and natives came to report that thousands of "little yellow men" were gathered at Point Taivu.

General Vandegrift decided to hit the enemy first and sent Edson's Raiders against the foe. Red Mike landed east of Point Taivu at dawn, September 8, with 850 men. He surprised Kawaguchi's sleepy rearguard and pounced on the main Japanese base at Tasimboko Village.

Covered by low-flying, strafing Army P-400's, and the shellfire of the destroyers that had transported them to Taivu, the Leathernecks drove Kawaguchi's men into the jungle. In Tasimboko, they blew up tons of small arms ammunition, dumped an artillery battery into the sea, and razed the supply depot by setting fire to the crammed warehouses.

The Raiders brought back souvenirs of their foray. The most highly prized one being a splendid white dress uniform that belonged to General Kawaguchi. He had planned to wear it the day he captured Henderson Field.

Leaving Tasimboko in flames, Edson's men boarded the

destroyers for an uneventful run back to Lunga Point where Kawaguchi's elegant uniform was put on display.

The quantities of supplies at Tasimboko convinced Vandegrift that several thousand enemy troops had been landed on Guadalcanal. Intelligence reports indicated they were marching through the jungle in the direction of Henderson Field. The question facing him was to determine where the main Japanese blow would fall.

Lacking manpower to reinforce every sector of his perimeter, the general strengthened those most vulnerable to attack from the south. After deploying his forces, Vandegrift noticed a hole in the perimeter east of the Lunga River. Studying the terrain, he saw, only a mile south of Henderson Field, a nameless ridge with *kunai* grass covered slopes, that stretched for a thousand yards in a northwest-southeast slant.

The Marine CO realized the ridge was the key to the defense of Henderson Field and hastily fortified it. He assigned the Raiders to defend what was immediately named "Edson's Ridge" (a name soon to be replaced by "Bloody Ridge" because of the gory battle that took place for its possession).

The Raiders were still digging in at daybreak, Saturday, September 12, when Kawaguchi's men burst out of the jungle and hurled themselves at the Marines.

As his infantry struck, enemy aircraft unleashed a blow the Japanese hoped would knock out the U.S. planes at

Henderson Field. Vals and Bettys escorted by Zekes swarmed above the vital airstrip only to be slaughtered by Army, Navy, and Marine fliers. Ten of the Mikado's "war eagles" tumbled out of the sky in minutes. The rest of the

THE FIGHT FOR BLOODY RIDGE

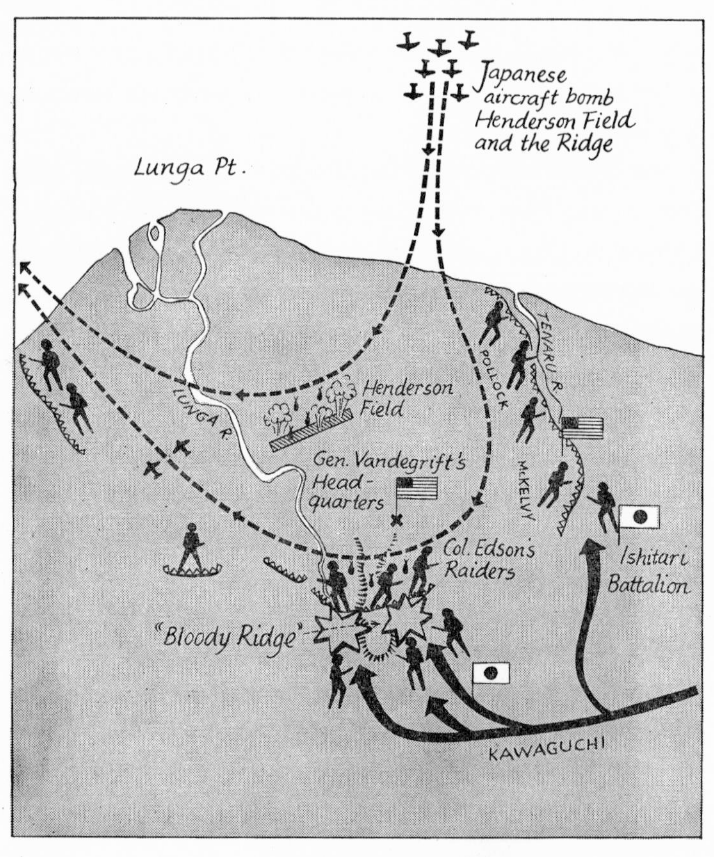

enemy planes fled to Rabaul but not until two Bettys had plastered the length of the Ridge with sticks of bombs.

"Those eggs didn't do any damage or even cause casualties," a Marine recalled. "The Nips did us a big favor by dropping them. They blasted out real fine foxholes along the spine of the Ridge."

The fighting was fierce all day, September 12, as Kawaguchi probed for weak spots. By nightfall, he ordered bayonet charges at various places, hoping for a breakthrough.

The Raiders held, although forced back at a few points. During the night men clashed and died in the darkness. Kawaguchi's soldiers fought bravely but could not dislodge the Marines who broke up the enemy's charges with mortars, machine guns, and rifles.

On September 13, Kawaguchi expected to raise the Rising Sun flag over Henderson Field despite the previous day's failures. He mounted numerous attacks to keep the Marines off balance while Henderson Field was subjected to daylong air raids.

Edson's men were hungry and battle-weary. The wounded received no medical care. Ammunition was running low. Some machine gunners were down to the last belt while riflemen had only a clip or two left.

"The Nips had us licked, but we wouldn't admit it," said one Marine, summing up the crisis on Bloody Ridge.

At nightfall, the Raiders braced for a final stand. Red

Mike Edson bluntly stated, "There's only us between the Japs and the airfield. If they take Henderson we'll lose The Canal!"

When daylight faded, the Marines crouched deeper in their foxholes. From the jungle they heard the Japanese cheering as officers exhorted them to "make the supreme sacrifice for the glory of the Emperor!"

General Kawaguchi informed the Imperial Staff by radio that "before another sunrise, Henderson Field will be in our hands." He even suggested Radio Tokyo should announce to the public that the American airfield had fallen.

Kawaguchi was certain the Marines could not withstand the assault he had readied against them. At midnight, one of his best units—the Ishitari Battalion—was to attack the Americans on the Tenaru River as he launched an all-out assault against Bloody Ridge, thus taking the Yankees in a pincers from the east and the south. He also arranged with Admiral Mikawa for a cruiser bombardment of Marine positions all the way from Lunga Point to the Tenaru.

The general regretted assaulting Bloody Ridge without proper artillery preparation, but the Raiders had tossed all his big guns into Sealark Channel during the raid on Tasimboko. Artillery or not, Kawaguchi meant to finish the job that Sunday night.

At 2230 (10:30 P.M.) the attack started in the usual fashion. A red rocket swooshed from the jungle to herald the onslaught. Mortar shells crashed on the ridge crest.

They had scarcely ceased exploding before infantrymen boiled out of the night and charged up the sides of the ridge.

Kawaguchi tried a new ruse this time. A cloud of green-tinged smoke billowed around the Marine positions on the left flank. "Gas! Run, Yanks, run! Poison gas!" shrieked a Japanese. But the Marines did not budge.

They recognized the thick clouds to be a smoke screen and not poison gas. As the veil drifted off, hundreds of Kawaguchi's soldiers rushed the Americans. Flares lighted their way and in the light, the Marines could see the enemy's bayonets and swords glinting.

The Raiders rose to meet the foe, but the impetus of the Japanese drive proved too much. Slowly, the Marines fell back, losing one position after another, until they had been squeezed onto a knoll less than a half-mile from Henderson Field.

As the American lines bent, Captain John B. Sweeney's Baker (B) Company was cut off from the main body. Sweeney had only 60 men left, but his survivors made a bayonet charge that slashed through the encirclement.

"We just busted out of there, yelling our fool heads off and jabbing Nips left and right," a participant recalled.

Captain Harry Torgerson, who had lost his pants while blasting the Japanese out of their caves on Tulagi, rallied his men with a string of oaths as they scampered towards the backslope of the ridge.

"Old Torgy called us everything under the sun and never

repeated a single word. We went back into the fight more scared of him than the Japs," a Marine said later.

The battle reached a gruesome climax. Machine guns mowed down Kawaguchi's men. Yet, whenever the attack seemed to be tapering off, red rockets lit the jungle and more Japanese leaped into the fray.

No man who fought the Kawaguchis that night would ever doubt the enemy's courage. "They were incredible," an American officer observed. "I never saw such bravery."

Some Japanese actually reached Henderson Field. Four, led by an officer brandishing a *samurai* sword, broke into the Division CP, located a quarter of a mile behind the front.

Shrieking *"Banzai!"* the quartet fell upon the CP staff. Startled Marines opened fire with their pistols and carbines. The infiltrators dropped dead at their feet, but not until the officer had killed a sergeant with his sword.

At one time, according to Lt. Col. Samuel Griffith, the Raiders' Executive Officer, the foe actually seized the ridge crest and ". . . would have held it, had not Colonel Edson called for artillery to knock them off . . . Our 75-mm pack howitzers let go . . . and the shells exploded right under our noses . . . If that artillery had been a hundred yards short, we'd have been blown to bits with the Japs. . . ."

The barrage either killed or drove away the Japanese on the crest. The artillery then lengthened its range and continued to pound the enemy. As the night waned, Kawaguchi's attacks weakened. By 0230 (2:30 A.M.) Edson was able to tell General Vandegrift that the Raiders could hold Bloody Ridge.

3

Precisely at midnight, when the battle on the ridge reached its peak, the Ishitari Battalion went into action against Blue Battalion, 1st Marines (Lt. Colonel W. N. McKelvy,

THE JAPANESE REPELLED

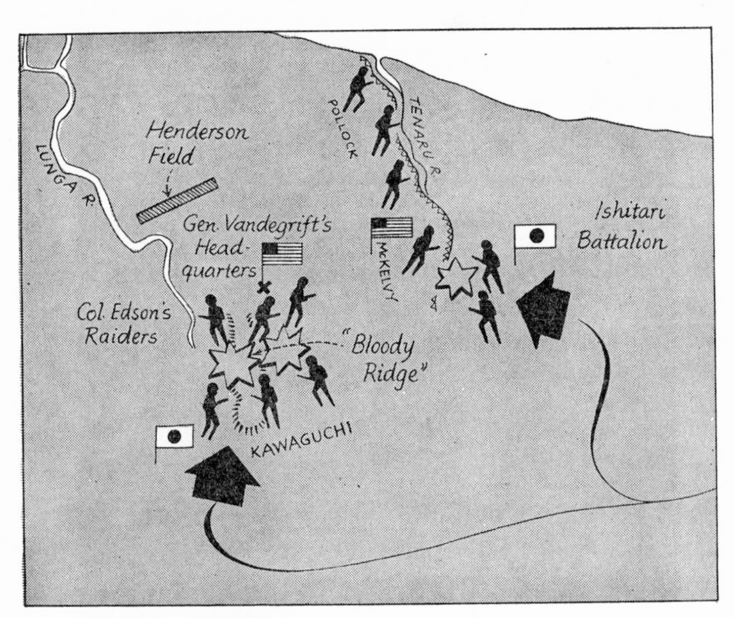

Jr.), manning the Tenaru River Line. The attackers were caught in Marine barbed wire entanglements and the charge was quickly smashed both by 75-mm pack howitzers and a tank-led counterattack.

While this repulse was taking place, Vice Admiral Gunichi Mikawa, the victor of Savo Island, arrived off Guadalcanal with his heavy cruisers. He waited for a signal from Kawaguchi before starting his bombardment.

A green flare was to indicate that Henderson Field had fallen. But no rocket came. Gun flashes and explosions ashore told Mikawa heavy fighting was going on. He lingered almost until dawn before retiring without firing a shot. If Henderson Field remained in American hands, Mikawa could not risk being caught by SBD's taking off from there. Obviously, Kawaguchi had failed.

At daybreak, the Marines looked down upon a ghastly sight from their hard-won positions atop Bloody Ridge. More than six hundred dead Japanese lay on the slope and also scores of the enemy had fallen within the U.S. perimeter.

Wildcats from Henderson Field strafed the retreating enemy at tree-top level. The beaten Kawaguchis plunged into the jungle and hacked out a trail westward to Kokumbona, leaving behind over 600 dead and 500 wounded in their abortive attempt to storm Bloody Ridge. (Official Japanese figures listed casualties at 633 killed and 505 wounded.) Another 250 men of the Ishitari Battalion died at the Tenaru River while more than 100 were killed by Blue Battalion, 5th Marines, which repulsed a third attack along the Matanikau River.

The Japanese suffered terribly on the retreat march through the jungle. One of Kawaguchi's staff officers described the ordeal in these words: "I cannot help crying when I see my men marching without food . . . carrying the wounded over the curving and sloping mountain trails. . . . The wounded received no medical attention . . . and many died in agony. . . ."

At last the emaciated remnants of the Kawaguchi Brigade stumbled into Kokumbona and Kawaguchi broke down when he saw these tottering ghosts. Of the 3,400 fighting men he had led onto Guadalcanal, more than half were lost. The Battle of Bloody Ridge was a terrific setback to the Japanese time table; not for more than a month would General Kawaguchi's men be able to take the field.

The Battle of Bloody Ridge was among the decisive ground actions in the Pacific War. Had the Marines lost, Guadalcanal would have been as bitter a defeat for the U.S. as were Pearl Harbor, Bataan, and Corregidor. Only the courage of individual Marines and the leadership shown by Col. Edson and his officers wrested the victory from a brave and determined enemy.

Although the Japanese had received a bad jolt, their spirit remained unbroken. A private of the Kawaguchi Brigade, one of the few prisoners captured at Bloody Ridge, standing amidst the bodies of his comrades, snarled at the Marines in English: "It matters nothing about all of us you killed! More will come! Many more! We will never stop until we have conquered!"

This was typical of the determination displayed by the stubborn soldiers of the Mikado, who were too proud to admit defeat.

CHAPTER SIX

The Night of the Battleships

OCTOBER 14, 1942

Six

1

After the Battle of Bloody Ridge, the Marines wondered what would happen next. The Leathernecks had many opinions about the enemy's future moves but were unanimous on one point. Help had better come soon. Malaria and other tropical diseases were depleting their ranks. It was estimated that three men in seven were suffering from malaria, dengue, or jungle rot. Almost every man had lost weight.

"We looked like a bunch of scarecrows," a Marine said.

Admiral Ghormley (Comsopac) knew the situation on Guadalcanal. He despatched reinforcements from Espiritu Santo to the Canal. On September 14, the 7th Marine Regiment set sail in a convoy guarded by destroyers, cruisers, two aircraft carriers (the *Wasp* and the *Hornet*), plus the battleship *North Carolina.*

Ghormley was aware that the waters around the Solomon Islands were patrolled by some twenty enemy submarines concentrated in the 640-mile-long stretch of the Coral Sea between Espiritu Santo and Guadalcanal.

American sailors called that region "Torpedo Junction" because of the many submarine attacks that took place there. In addition to danger from undersea craft, U.S. Naval Intelligence reported enemy battleships and carriers concentrated somewhere north of the Santa Cruz Islands. Japanese bombers on Rabaul and Bougainville also menaced the shipping between Espiritu Santo and Guadalcanal. Despite these perils Comsopac had to act. The Marines on Guadalcanal had to be reinforced at any cost.

"Torpedo Junction" proved its reputation on September 15, which was a black day for the U.S. Navy. At sunrise, the Japanese submarine *I-19* put a spread of torpedoes into the *Wasp*. The flattop, shattered by a series of explosions, was enshrouded in flames. She went down, after burning all day, with a loss of 193 killed and 366 wounded. Fortunately, she had launched all but a few of her aircraft just before getting hit. The planes landed safely on the *Hornet* which sped out of danger followed by her own destroyers and cruisers as well as the *Wasp's*.

Shortly after the flattop was hit, another enemy submarine badly damaged the *North Carolina* and destroyer *O'Brien*. The battleship managed to make Espiritu Santo and after some patchwork limped back to Pearl Harbor for repairs.

The Japanese gloated over sinking the *Wasp* and crippling the *North Carolina.* Only hours after the *I-19* had killed the carrier, a rally was held in Tokyo at the huge Hinomiya Sports Stadium.

There, high-ranking Imperial Army and Navy officers told cheering thousands that an American carrier ". . . has been eliminated . . . along with a battleship and other ships. . . . It is a glorious moment for the Imperial Navy!"

Not to be outdone, the Army won its share of applause when a staff colonel in full dress uniform proudly announced that the Guadalcanal airfield had been retaken and ". . . 10,000 American Marines, mercenaries hired by the gangster Roosevelt, will soon be exterminated. . . ."

Joyous civilians snake-danced through Tokyo's streets waving flags, singing, shouting *banzai* and chanting patriotic slogans until far into the night. At the Imperial General Staff headquarters, smiling officers drank *sake* to the victories on land and at sea.

The officers lifting high their *sake* cups to toast the "recapture" of Henderson Field and the "extermination" of the Marines knew these claims were untrue.

Each was aware what had befallen the Kawaguchi Brigade on Bloody Ridge, the Tenaru, and the Matanikau. But their elaborate pretence had to do with the Oriental custom of "saving face." It must have been strange to see the otherwise realistic staff officers playing a game of self-delusion.

The situation became ludicrous when General Hyakutate received a flood of congratulatory messages from his superiors for having ". . . planned and carried out the destruction of American forces in the Solomon Islands . . ."

However, the Japanese could not long continue their fantasies. The U.S. Marines were not wiped out. Henderson Field was not captured and despite the Imperial submarines, the 4,000 men of the 7th Marine Regiment had landed at Lunga Point on September 18, with all their tanks, jeeps, medical supplies, arms, rations, ammunition, and artillery.

2

After the 7th Marines arrived, more than 20,000 Leathernecks defended the perimeters. They improved the positions; dirt flew as rifle platoons dug deep foxholes, and machine gun crews prepared new emplacements. Mortars covered the trails to Henderson Field, which Vandegrift felt would be the focal point of any Japanese attack.

Barbed wire was strung in row after row until the hooked strands were interlaced like spider webs in front of every position. The Marines rigged booby traps, cleverly set off by concealed trip wires. General Vandegrift lived up to his standards of thoroughness. No defensive detail was ignored. When the enemy again attacked Henderson Field, he would find the Americans ready.

The island war stalled. Neither side made any significant moves. But, every day, men were killed and wounded in unimportant clashes. Sometimes the Marines lured a Japanese patrol into an ambush. Sometimes it was the Americans who were tricked.

Although ground action was nearly at a standstill, the air war raged unabated. The Henderson Field fliers—now officially known as Cactus Air Force because the Guadalcanal campaign bore the code name "Operation Cactus" —had become adept at destroying Japanese planes. From the Marines' landing, August 7, until the end of September, U.S. pilots downed over 200 Japanese planes with a loss of only 32 to themselves.

Cactus Air Force had been brought to this peak by its CO, Major General Roy Geiger, who had taken command early in September. The fiery general was an officer who led by example. Fifty-seven-year-old Geiger, a veteran of World War I, took up a Dauntless on September 22 to guide a night strike against the "Tokyo Express," just to show his young pilots how he wanted things done.

But even General Geiger could not stop the "Tokyo Express." The enemy continued to pour men and supplies onto Gaudalcanal and built up a big base at Kokumbona, west of the Matanikau River. The troops being put ashore were from the Sendai Division, the flower of the Imperial Army.

The Sendais had been sent to Guadalcanal because the Imperial General Staff officers finally faced facts. The only way to drive the U.S. Marines off the island, they agreed, was by a massive attack using thousands of troops. The 20,000-man Sendai Division was tapped for that task and General Hyakutate received orders directing him to ". . . engage the enemy at once and eliminate him by mid-October."

The general prepared what became known as the "Hyakutate Extermination Plan." It called for advance elements of the Sendai Division to be rushed by destroyers to Kokumbona. Once the division was established there, Lt. General Masao Maruyama, the Sendai CO, and his staff, would follow to conduct the offensive.

The Division's main body, aboard slower transports, and guarded by air and sea power, was then scheduled to arrive. Finally, in early October, Hyakutate would journey to Guadalcanal to be present for the American surrender.

The 17th Army CO issued the necessary orders and on Monday, September 21, the advance guard of the Sendai Division boarded destroyers at Rabaul as the spearhead for the "magnificent victory" General Hyakutate predicted they would win, in a special order read to the men before they embarked at Rabaul.

3

The Japanese buildup west of the Matanikau River forced General Vandergrift to attack before the enemy got too strong. The terrain where the Marine offensive would be launched, was better suited for defense than attack. There were steep, jungle-covered hills, ridges and deeply wooded ravines.

On September 23, General Vandegrift ordered Lt. Col. Lewis "Chesty" Puller to march Red Battalion, 7th Marines, into the hills south and west of Henderson Field on a reconnaissance-in-force.

This mission, scheduled to last until September 26, was to be followed up by the 1st Raider Battalion crossing the Matanikau River at its mouth and seizing Kokumbona Village. Both moves were merely preliminaries to Vandegrift's main offensive, a full-scale assault to "wipe out enemy forces concentrated beyond the Matanikau . . ."

A Marine 1st Division staff officer explained the operation in these terms: "We'll give the Jap a one-two punch to throw him off balance . . . and then follow through with a haymaker . . ."

This was an apt description of the American plan, but the Japanese rolled with the punches and hit back hard. The Marines ran into trouble at the outset. Puller disappeared into the jungle south of Henderson Field and was not heard from for an entire day, while Vandegrift waited impatiently for news.

At last, on the night of September 24, Red Battalion stretcher bearers brought in twenty-five wounded men. They had stumbled into a Japanese ambush near Grassy Knoll.

Not knowing the enemy's strength, Puller had halted until he received instructions from Vandegrift whether to press on until he reached the Matanikau or to fall back at once.

Vandegrift sent Puller White Battalion, 5th Marines, as reinforcements and gave him leeway to advance or retreat at his own discretion. As the general had anticipated, Puller elected to move ahead.

He reached the Matanikau on the 25th, but was repulsed by strong enemy resistance when attempting to cross it. The Japanese also beat off attacks by the 1st Raider Battalion and the Marines had to retreat. The fruitless offensive ended when Vandegrift pulled his units from the Matanikau and had them dig in about a mile from the river bank.

The operation had been poorly planned and badly carried out. The attack cost the Marines 60 killed and 100 wounded with nothing gained after four days of combat. The defeat wound up the second month the Marines had been on Guadalcanal; it was a dismal episode on that unhappy island, but with the coming of October, far worse things lay ahead for the Americans.

4

The weather changed during the first week in October—it became more unbearable. The rains, diseases, and miseries increased.

Every night the Marines peered out of foxholes wondering when a red rocket would arch above the trees to signal an attack. They knew the lull could not last much longer. The "Tokyo Express" was disgorging about 900 Sendais nightly. Soon, the enemy's strength would be at its peak and then he would unleash his force on the Americans.

The time was closer than the Marines guessed. On October 4, the "Tokyo Express" had landed an important passenger, Lt. General Masao Maruyama, CO of the Sendai Division.

Even in the strictly disciplined Imperial Army, this haughty man was noted as a martinet. Easily irritated, he had a hair-trigger temper. Maruyama saw much on Guadalcanal to displease him. The main target of his anger was Colonel Akinosuke Oka, who commanded the troops west of the Matanikau River.

The general berated Oka for letting the Americans get away during the recent fighting at the river. He also reprimanded the colonel for permitting fresh Sendai troops to mingle with survivors of the Kawaguchi Brigade and the Ichiki Detachment.

The first Sendais to reach Guadalcanal, the 4th Regiment, had been issued new weapons, uniforms, camouflage helmet cover, mosquito netting, and split-toed shoes. The 4th carried Class "A" rations: tinned fish and beef, canned vegetables, even hard candies. There was a supply of *sake* for officers and rice beer for enlisted men.

Compared to the ravaged Kawaguchi and Ichiki veterans, the Sendais were like supermen—strong, vigorous, and healthy. Colonel Oka had bivouacked the newcomers near the old-timers. Kawaguchis and Ichikis tottered into the 4th Regiment's camp begging for food, beer, and candy.

They told the Sendais of conditions on the island and filled them with tales about the ferocity of the U.S. Marines. The stories shocked and depressed Maruyama's men. They had been led to believe the Americans were cowards and that the campaign would be easy. Morale in the 4th Regiment sagged when the troops learned the truth.

One man wrote in his diary: "Who can bear such horrors as we have heard? I am fearful . . . What the Kawaguchis and Ichikis tell us is not for human ears . . ."

Another confided to his journal: "I tremble when I think of the Marines. What beasts they must be! If I go into battle I fear that I will disgrace my Emperor, my country, and my ancestors! Before that takes place I shall destroy myself . . ."

According to an aide, General Maruyama "raved like a madman" when he found how demoralized his men had become. "The General shouted at Oka until his voice grew hoarse," the officer wrote later. "I found it in my heart to feel sorry for the colonel, standing at attention under such abuse. But he took it well and when General Maruyama dismissed him, marched away like a soldier."

It was rumored Oka would commit *hara-kiri*. By ancient

samurai tradition, he could wipe out the disgrace of his public scolding only by killing himself. Colonel Oka had probably outgrown the customs of the past for he made no move toward self-destruction and continued with his duties as though nothing unusual had taken place.

General Maruyama decided the way to lift his men's spirits was with an inspirational message. He said, in part:

"Soldiers of Japan! The coming battle will decide the fate of our nation! If we do not succeed in occupying this island, let no man expect to get home alive! The honor of the Emperor demands either success or our lives! *Banzai!*"

Maruyama's words made the Sendais unhappier than ever but they now knew the general meant business. After all, death in battle was the sworn obligation of every Japanese soldier. "Better to die for the Mikado than live a hundred years" was the credo of the Imperial Army.

Maruyama next settled down to formulating a plan for the campaign of extermination. Two more regiments, the 16th and the 29th, heavy artillery, and a naval landing force several thousand strong, were soon coming to him via the Tokyo Express. Maruyama would be ready when these reinforcements arrived at Kokumbona.

In the meantime, he decided to seize the eastern bank of the Matanakau River as a jumping-off sector for his big push. He ordered Colonel Juro Nakaguma to take the 4th Regiment across at daybreak, Wednesday, October 7.

As Maruyama studied the maps, he even selected the

place to which General Vandegrift must be taken on October 15, for surrender ceremonies. While the 4th Regiment prepared to cross the Matanikau, General Vandegrift decided he no longer could stand by while the enemy was building up west of the river. The Marines had to span the Matanikau and scatter the Japanese concentrations.

The Marine general, after his September defeat, decided to use larger forces in any new offensive he undertook. For this one, he picked five battalions jointly led by Red Mike Edson, now commanding the 5th Marines, and Col. William "Wild Bill" Whaling, CO, Blue Battalion, 2nd Marines.

General Vandegrift chose to launch his attack at daybreak, Wednesday, October 7.

5

The Japanese and the Americans were on a collision course. They crashed early October 7, when Blue Battalion, 5th Marines, reached the mouth of the Matanikau River and started over just as Colonel Nakaguma's advance guard, three companies strong, came to the river. A bitter fight broke out between these forces. It roared up and down the river line and the Japanese were winning until Edson radioed for help.

Vandegrift rushed up Red Mike's old command, the 1st Raider Battalion. It was depleted to a skeleton unit by death, wounds, battle fatigue, and disease. Although they already had given so much, the Raiders put out a little more, drove Nakaguma's men into a pocket and when the Japanese tried to break out that night, killed them to the last man.

A short distance upriver, Colonel Whaling's men went over the Matanikau on a span of logs the Marines called Nippon Bridge. Once his troops reached the river's western bank, Whaling swung toward the sea to link up with Edson. The Americans had established firm footholds on both sides of the river.

General Vandegrift had to halt operations the next day (October 8) when a great rainstorm broke over Guadalcanal. Water poured like a cataract from a sky, so black, according to one Marine, that ". . . men had to grope in

ATTACK AT THE MATANIKAU

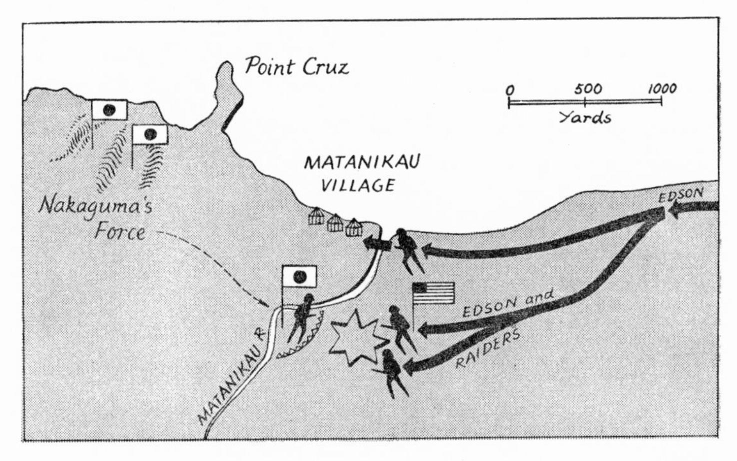

the jungle as though they were at the bottom of a coal pit . . ." That day, all Guadalcanal was "a sea of mud" and no fighting took place.

On October 9, a scorching sun baked the ground hard and dry and the war could continue. At an early hour, Intelligence received word of a huge enemy invasion force making ready at Rabaul. On the strength of this report Vandegrift determined not to drive any farther west but to pull back and fortify the Matanikau's eastern bank against the certain Japanese offensive.

As a parting shot he ordered Col. Whaling to join Edson, hit the enemy troops near Matanikau Village, and recross the river to the eastern side. Edson started towards Matanikau Village along with White Battalion, 7th Marines (Lt. Col. Herman Hanneken). Edson and Hanneken advanced without meeting resistance. No Japanese were found by Whaling on his march to Matanikau Village.

This lack of opposition made all three officers suspicious. Were they moving into a trap? Edson, Hanneken, and Whaling joined forces at the coastal road, but before pushing toward the village, they sent Lt. Colonel Chesty Puller on a reconnaissance with Red Battalion, 7th Marines. Puller left the road and probed the jungle in a straight line to Point Cruz.

He found the Japanese.

As his men toiled along a jungle-blanketed ridge, he halted the column. A ravine below swarmed with enemy soldiers—a full battalion of Nakaguma's 4th Regiment —deployed off the coastal road near Matanikau Village to ambush the Marines coming along that route.

Nakaguma apparently had overlooked the possibility that the Americans might sneak up on him through the jungle. Puller's battalion moved undetected atop their ridge. Machine guns and mortars were placed to enfilade the enemy. Riflemen crawled into line and when all was ready, Puller gave the signal to open fire.

Mortars and machine guns raked the Japanese. The enemy could not escape the avalanche of lead. The ravine became a slaughter pen. The Japanese clawed at the rocky slopes to climb the ridge, but Puller's machine gunners and

PULLER'S AMBUSH

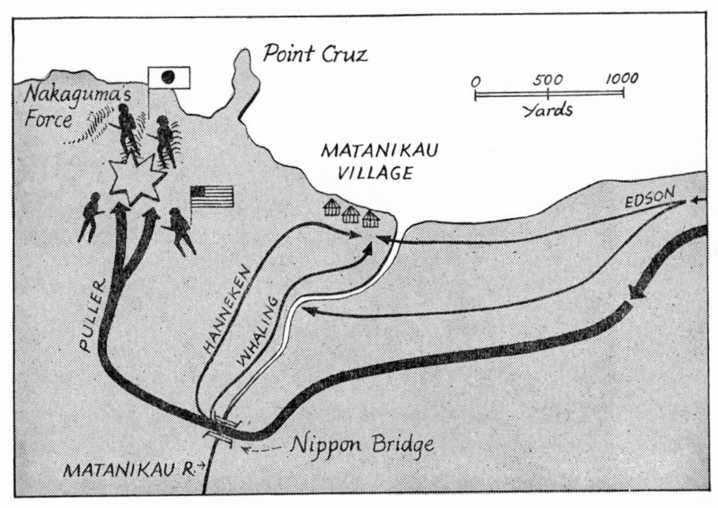

riflemen drove Nakaguma's men back into the death trap.

Some Japanese tried to escape by running to the end of the ravine and climbing an opposite ridge. But Puller rushed a company to the second ridge and the fleeing foe only blundered into another ambush.

Puller radioed for artillery and air strikes. Fiery death raked and re-raked that defile. Wildcats swooped with machine guns blazing. Heavy-caliber shells swept every foot. At last there were no more targets left; only the dead occupied that place. Puller's Marines stared down in horror; they had slaughtered 690 of the Mikado's best troops.

"It was a big victory," a Marine said. "But from where we stood, it looked like mass murder. I felt sorry for the Japs; that was no way to die. But it was war; they'd have done the same thing to us. I can remember thinking: 'How much longer will we have to keep doing this kind of thing?' "

Edson, Whaling, and Hanneken later broke into Matanikau Village and killed another 200 soldiers of the unlucky 4th Regiment. The survivors would have horror stories of their own to tell the reinforcements landing on Guadalcanal, which Japanese enlisted men had begun to call Death Island.

6

General Vandegrift exploited his victories of October 7–9. Sending all available troops to guard the Matanikau River crossings, he also kept a tight defensive perimeter around Henderson Field.

The Americans no longer had to fear an enemy thrust from the Tenaru River in the east. As Puller was destroying Nakaguma's battalion, a detachment from the 2nd Marines eliminated the last Japanese force in the Tenaru sector.

Vandegrift's main concern was the enemy fleet plowing through the Slot. He would have been even more troubled had he known that aboard a cargo vessel were four long range 150-mm howitzers with which Maruyama intended to blast Henderson Field at a range of 12–15 miles.

These big guns were the general's ace-in-the-hole. No weapons of that size were on Guadalcanal. Maruyama was confident he could knock out Henderson Field with his heavy artillery. The big Japanese convoy, guarded by destroyers and cruisers, carried the final units of the Sendai Division and many tons of necessary supplies.

But the Americans did not intend to let the Japanese ships enter Ironbottom Sound unchallenged. Awaiting them off Cape Esperance was Rear Admiral Norman Scott with four cruisers and five destroyers.

On the night of October 11–12, Scott pounced upon the Japanese in the same general area where the Five Sitting Ducks had been massacred. By executing a complicated maneuver, Scott swung his task force broadside to the approaching enemy and loosed a murderous barrage.

His flagship, the heavy cruiser *San Francisco,* and her sister ship *Salt Lake City,* registered hits. The Imperial Navy's cruiser *Furutaka* broke in half and went down. The *Aoba,* flagship of Rear Admiral Aritomo Goto, was gutted by forty shells. Half her crew was killed and on the shattered bridge, Goto, riddled by shell splinters, bled to death.

The engagement became a free-for-all. Ships blasted at any target in the darkness and friends sometimes fired at each other. The large Japanese destroyer *Fubuki* joined the dead ships on the floor of Ironbottom Sound. The Amer-

NAVAL FIGHT OFF CAPE ESPERANCE

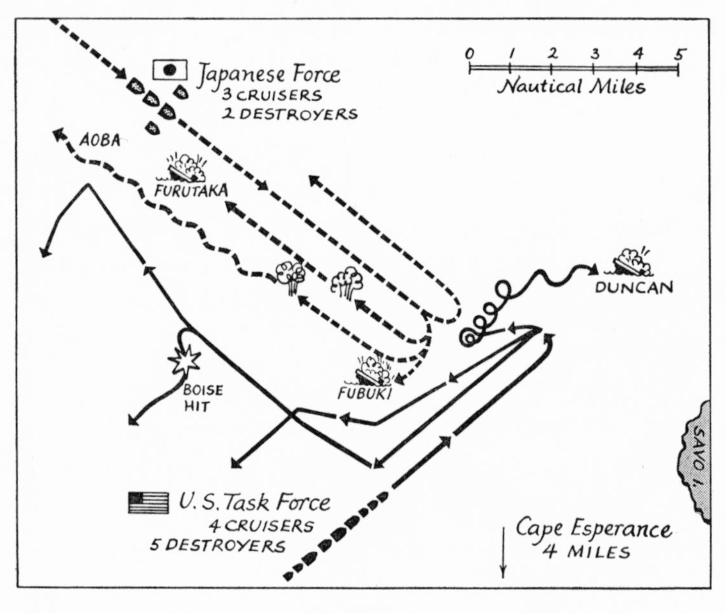

ican destroyer *Duncan* plunged beneath the waves. Two gun turrets on the U.S. cruiser *Boise* were battered into twisted wreckage.

The Americans were not done with the Japanese ships. At daybreak Monday (October 12), SBD's from Henderson Field streaked up into the morning sky, found the enemy destroyers *Murakumo* and *Natsugumo* and sank them with 1,000 pound bombs. There were broad smiles on Guadalcanal when the results of the naval battle off Cape Esperance were announced.

U.S. jubilation was somewhat lessened as Intelligence announced that during the sea battle, sizeable enemy troop reinforcements had landed at Kokumbona. The four 150-mm guns, soon to be nicknamed "Pistol Petes" by the Marines, had also been brought safely ashore.

The major result of the Battle of Cape Esperance was to bolster American morale. Now Japanese ships also littered the floor of Ironbottom Sound. Most important, the U.S. Navy had won a night engagement. "The Japs had us flustered. We thought they were our masters at night fighting. After Cape Esperance we saw they could be taken," a Navy officer stated at the time.

The Japanese had a philosophical explanation for their defeat. "Providence abandoned us and our losses mounted. Perhaps we had grown too confident and needed to be reminded that humbleness is a virtue," an Imperial Navy report observed.

7

On Tuesday, October 13, while they were still rejoicing over the Cape Esperance victory, the Marines at Lunga Point saw a line of gray-painted cargo ships steaming up Sealark Channel. They were Admiral Turner's transports carrying supplies, rations, and the 164th Infantry Regiment, Americal Division, U.S. Army. The Marines had long been hearing scuttlebutt that the army was on the way. However, the Leathernecks discounted the rumors and even composed a song about the army to the melody of "Bless 'em All!":

> "We asked all the Doggies
> To come to Tulagi,
> But General MacArthur said 'No'—
> When asked for his reason—
> 'It isn't the season.
> 'Besides you have no U.S.O.!' "

Now the Leathernecks had to swallow their own words for off the landing barges splashed 3,000 GIs in full battle gear. The Marines jeered at the soldiers but beneath their scorn were glad to see the "dogfaces."

Most pleased of all the Marines who watched the ships arrive were the handful left in the 1st Raider Battalion. When the transports went back to Nouméa, the Raiders were scheduled to return aboard them. The battalion's tour on The Canal was ended. Probably every Marine present envied the Raiders for being permitted to leave Guadalcanal—but no man begrudged their good fortune. When the Raiders stumbled aboard the ships, it was with the cheers of those who stayed behind.

At about noon, something louder than cheers sounded over Lunga Point and Henderson Field as 24 Japanese bombers flying very high, made an unopposed run over the airfield and scored hits. The attack was one of the most successful staged by Imperial aircraft.

The Kates set afire many tons of aviation gasoline and other supplies. A second wave blasted the field again, while a third flight worked over the area where the 164th Infantry was bivouacked. Even before they were properly settled in, the GIs learned the facts of life and death on The Canal.

Henderson Field had received no advance warning about the enemy bombers because the Japanese had launched a campaign against the coastwatchers. Those valiant men had to flee their posts with the result that Henderson Field took a pasting that afternoon.

However, the engineers soon filled in the bomb craters that pock-marked the runway while firefighters extinguished the flames. Henderson Field was back in operation before sunset. Then, at dusk, the Japanese threw their newest weapon into the fray. Just as the Marines were eating chow, there was a screeching overhead followed by a blast that shook the earth. Another explosion, and then another, gouged fresh holes on the airstrip. The air raid sirens sounded and everyone dashed for foxholes, bomb shelters, and slit trenches.

After a while, Marines and GIs realized this was not an air attack but an artillery bombardment. The 150-mm howitzers—the "Pistol Petes"—were shelling Henderson Field from west of the Matanikau, more than 12 miles away.

The barrage continued with accuracy. A Marine storehouse blew up. An ammunition dump exploded. The Marines guarding the perimeter were subjected to a pounding. The 164th Infantry took such punishment that a platoon sergeant went mad and crawled around in the open begging someone to shoot him.

The "Pistol Petes" kept hammering away until the U.S. destroyers *Sterett, Gwin,* and *Nicholas* opened a counter barrage on the gun positions and the 150's fell silent. It was dark by the time the shelling stopped, and dazed Americans crept out of their holes.

Repair work started as soon as the shelling was over. The Marines and GIs relaxed after the strain of the bombardment. They wondered if "Pistol Pete" had been knocked out by the destroyers. Most believed the enemy was "playing possum" and would hit them again. The troops argued whether aerial bombing or artillery was worse; around midnight everyone turned in for some sleep.

But only the dead slept on Guadalcanal that night.

8

Because the coastwatchers were on the run, the Americans did not know that the *Haruna* and the *Kongo,* two of the mightiest battleships in the Imperial Navy, accompanied by a swarm of cruisers and destroyers, were en route to Guadalcanal from Rabaul.

Aboard his flagship the *Kongo,* Vice Admiral Takeo Kurita, Combat Division 3, checked last-minute details of the mission to be carried out by his battle-wagons. Aided by his smaller ships, he was to stand off Lunga Point and pulverize Henderson Field with his 14-inch guns.

The battleships, screened by the cruiser *Isuzu* and eight destroyers, entered Ironbottom Sound undetected in the clouded night. (At the same time, another group of Japanese vessels, including transports and cargo ships, was making a regular "Tokyo Express" delivery of men and supplies at Tassafaronga, between Cape Esperance and Point Cruz, west of Kokumbona Village.)

The throbbing motor of a Japanese plane chugged over Henderson Field. "It's only 'Louie the Louse,' " veterans mumbled and went back to sleep. But "Louie the Louse" had an unpleasant surprise for them that night.

At 0100 (1:00 A.M.) October 14, he dropped flares and Henderson Field was clearly outlined in the bright, unwinking light. Moments later, earthquake explosions shook the Americans awake. Great sheets of fire engulfed

Henderson Field as the *Haruna* and the *Kongo* let loose salvos of 14-inch HE shells.

"Condition Red! Condition Red!" squawked the Marine alarm.

No one needed to be told there was trouble. The battleships' shells came rushing in with a noise "like a string of freight cars" and went off with "the thunder of Judgment Day," according to an eyewitness.

THE NIGHT OF THE BATTLESHIPS

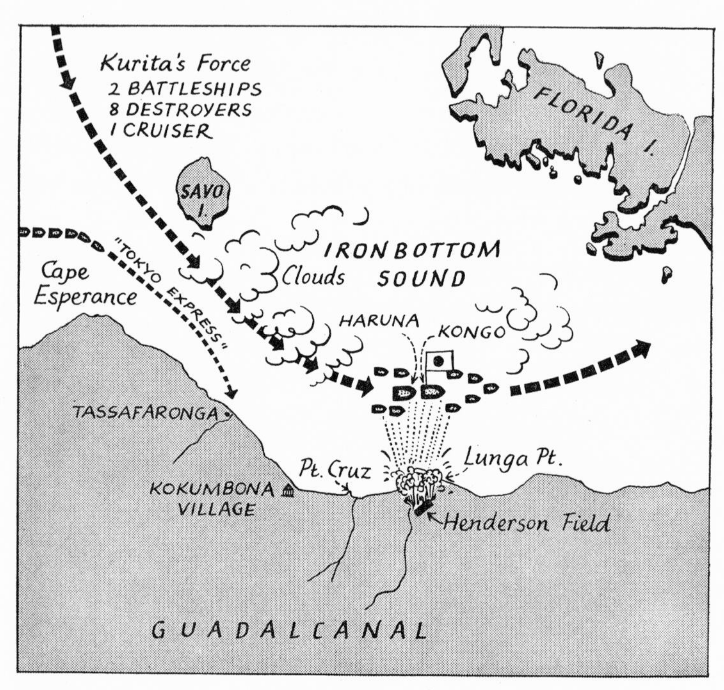

Nothing before on Guadalcanal compared to the shelling by the battleships, cruisers, and destroyers. Geysers of dirt rose high in the air. Trees were unrooted. Men were buried alive when their foxholes and shelters collapsed. Bombers and fighters were blasted into flaming bits. On the bridge of the *Kongo,* decorous Admiral Kurita grinned.

"The American airfield was a seething mass of fire; a sea of flames," one of his officers jotted in his diary. "We were convinced nothing could withstand that inferno."

For the 80-minute duration of the bombardment, most Americans cowering under the punishment would have agreed.

At 0230 (2:30 A.M.) with his ammunition almost expended, Kurita signaled the ships to cease fire. The battleships and their escorts sailed away, leaving Henderson Field in a shambles. Admiral Kurita was positive he had crippled it permanently.

The "Night of the Battleships" had ended. The situation at Henderson Field was worse than it had been during the critical days at the beginning of the campaign. Most of the aviation gas had been destroyed, and of the 90 planes on Henderson Field before the bombardment, only 35 fighters and seven dive-bombers remained undamaged.

Just after daylight (October 15) the four "Pistol Petes" again began shelling the Americans from their emplacements at the Matanikau and caused additional damage. Two waves of Japanese bombers lambasted the smoldering airstrip, but after the pummeling by Kurita's big guns, all this seemed mild.

At about 0800 (8:00 A.M.) a Marine colonel came to Henderson Field where repair and salvage crews were hard at work trying to patch up crippled aircraft. He assembled the pilots of the 67th Fighter Squadron and read them a statement from General Geiger:

> "We don't know whether we'll be able to hold the field or not. There's a Japanese task force of destroyers, cruisers and troop transports headed our way. We have enough gas left for one mission against them. Load your planes with bombs and go out with the dive-bombers and hit them. After the gas is gone we'll have to let the ground troops take over. Then your officers and men will attach themselves to some infantry outfit. Good luck and goodbye."

And as this grave notice was being read, an orderly handed an intercepted Marine radio message to Admiral Kurita. "Last night . . . we received a terrific bombardment from surface ships." The admiral permitted himself the luxury of a wide grin. Now he was positive the Yankees had been hurt.

CHAPTER SEVEN

Henderson Field

OCTOBER 19, 1942—

OCTOBER 26, 1942

Seven

1

The "Night of the Battleships" shook the Americans. The bombardment had come so close after the Japanese defeats on the Matanikau and off Cape Esperance that it seemed the enemy had unlimited resources.

"No matter how hard we slugged them, the Nips came back stronger than ever," a 1st Marine Division officer observed. "We were pretty well discouraged and disgusted."

This pessimism drifted back from Guadalcanal to Pearl Harbor where Admiral Chester Nimitz declared on October 15: "It now appears we are unable to control the sea in the Guadalcanal area. Thus our supply of the positions will only be done at great cost to us. The situation is not yet hopeless, but it is certainly critical."

The gloom over Guadalcanal reached the highest quarters. A few days after Nimitz had made his doleful statement, Secretary of the Navy Frank Knox was asked by reporters whether the U.S. forces could hold Guadalcanal. Knox shook his head, he ". . . would not make any prediction, but every man will give a good account of himself. . . . Everybody hopes that we can hold on. . . ."

The Yanks on The Canal might have conceded defeat but for General Vandegrift who refused to admit he was licked. He kept his men at work stringing barbed wire, laying mines, and booby traps, digging machine gun emplacements, and on constant patrol against a surprise attack.

General Geiger also would not give up. He got busy making Cactus Air Force a fighting unit again. A hurry call to Nouméa brought in six Dauntless bombers while a search uncovered 400 drums of gasoline that had been buried at the edge of the field back in August. Although work parties put the Henderson Field runway back into usable condition, the Americans had more bad news on the way. On October 14, the reserves of General Hyakutate's 17th Army were spotted in the Slot aboard six transports protected by destroyers and a swarm of Zeros. Cactus Air Force hit this convoy with four SBDs and seven Wildcats, but nicked only one destroyer.

That night (October 15–16), Admiral Gunichi Mikawa brought his flagship *Chokai* and the heavy cruiser *Kinugasa* into Sealark Channel and pumped more than 700 eight-inch shells upon Henderson Field.

On top of this, Marine outposts reported at daybreak on October 16 that the Japanese were unloading men and materiel at Tassafaronga from their half-dozen cargo vessels.

General Geiger was no man to wring his hands. He ordered every plane that could fly into the air. "Hit the Japs! Keep hitting them until you're out of bullets, bombs, or gas!" Geiger told the pilots.

Marine and Army fliers in patched Wildcats and SBDs held together by "spit, glue, and prayers" headed for Tassafaronga to strafe and bomb the transports. They caught the Japanese napping, for Admiral Mikawa had assured the transport commander that Henderson Field was "a graveyard of American planes."

However, the dead had arisen. Cactus Air Force, resurrected, not by miracles, but the hard work and skill of Henderson Field mechanics, still packed a punch.

The SBDs plastered the anchored transports with 1,000 and 500 pound bombs. The Wildcats came down to mast top height, strafing troops, and shooting up supplies stacked on the beach. Dogfights with Zeros raged in the blue, while tracer bullets and AA shells streaked and dotted the sky. That day, nothing could stop the Americans.

Not all of them were lucky. Young Lieutenant Anthony Turtora, an SBD pilot, had written his parents, "Always pray, not that I shall come back, but that I will have the courage to do my duty." He had the courage that morning of October 16.

He flew to Tassafaronga and dived to the attack; his

plane was hit, crashing in flames—one of three SBDs and four fighters lost by the Americans during an action that lasted many hours until after sunset.

But Lt. Turtora had not died in vain. Cactus Air Force had a fine day's hunting; with bombs and torpedoes it destroyed three big transports still carrying supplies.

The Japanese had trouble over Henderson Field as well as at Tassafaronga that day. Twelve enemy bombers and five of their fighters fell to AA guns and Wildcats in the course of numerous unsuccessful sorties by the foe.

By 1550 (3:50 P.M.) the commander of the Japanese transports at Tassafaronga decided to pull out before he lost all his ships. Three fully laden cargo vessels had already gone to the bottom. The remaining ones were damaged and all his destroyers had been hit. The surviving ships sped off at his signal. Marines watching from the ridges, whooped and shouted like spectators at a football game as Cactus Air Force planes executed victory loops in the darkening sky.

2

The devastating American aerial strike at Tassafaronga upset Lt. General Masao Maruyama. He flew into a rage against his staff officers as though they were responsible for losing the supply ships.

Maruyama had reason to be furious. He now had more than 20,000 soldiers on Guadalcanal, but much of their food, ammunition, and medical stores was at the bottom with the transports.

At last his anger burned out and the general took some solace from a punishing bombardment of American positions that night (October 16) by the heavy cruisers *Myoko* and *Maya*. The ships poured 1,500 eight-inch shells upon Henderson Field and the Marine perimeter.

The two cruisers wrought a lot of damage and General Geiger was able to muster only 25 bombers and nine fighters on October 17. Cactus Air Force was in bad shape again. A hurry call by Geiger brought 19 Wildcats and seven Dauntless bombers of Bomber Squadron 212, whose CO, Lt. Colonel Harold (Joe) Bauer, was a top Marine Corps fighter pilot with seven kills to his credit. The reinforcements reached The Canal as a flight of Aichi-99 (Val) dive-bombers were attacking Henderson Field and U.S. ships in Sealark Channel.

Bauer peeled off and went after eight Vals about to pounce on a destroyer. Within seconds, he had shot down four of them, driven off the rest and saved the destroyer. The mechanics found that the fuel tank of Bauer's Wildcat was completely empty when he landed on the pitted runway.

Mechanics and airmen swarmed around to congratulate him for his feat. He shrugged off their praise and growled,

"With a couple more pints of gas I could've knocked off the whole batch." This deed won for Bauer the Congressional Medal of Honor and brought his score of downed Japanese planes to eleven.

Despite the defeats they had suffered the Japanese decided to throw more strength on to Guadalcanal. By mid-October, recapturing that island obsessed the Imperial General Staff. Top-ranking Japanese admirals and generals were assigned to Operation KA. The Guadalcanal battle had to be won for the sake of Japanese morale. Australian and American troops had crushed the Port Moresby offensive, the New Guinea campaign had failed, and the Imperial Staff needed a victory.

Men, munitions, planes, and ships originally intended for Port Moresby were diverted to the Guadalcanal campaign. Operation KA received the highest priorities. General Hyakutate was no longer displeased with his assignment to the Solomons. At a conference held in Truk, Fleet Admiral Isoroku Yamamoto informed the general that the Combined Fleet was at his disposal.

It was an awesome mobilization of sea power: four aircraft carriers, four battleships, eight cruisers, 28 destroyers, and many auxiliary ships under the dual command of Vice Admirals Chuichi Nagumo and Nobutake Kondo. In addition, Yamamoto promised Hyakutate that the 17th Army would get everything needed for a successful termination of the Guadalcanal struggle.

Assured of full support, General Hyakutate decided to conduct the Guadalcanal operation in person. He arrived there from Rabaul on October 17, and went at once to Maruyama's headquarters at Kokumbona where he reviewed the battle plan his subordinate had drawn up.

Maruyama's plan called for a three-pronged land assault: two big attacks across the Matanikau and a third aimed at Henderson Field from the south while the Combined Fleet swept the U.S. Navy from adjacent waters and launched carrier-borne aircraft to paralyze Henderson Field.

The opening blow of the offensive would be delivered by Colonel Akinosuke Oka, who was to cross the Matanikau near Nippon Bridge on October 20 and outflank U.S. positions along the river.

At the same time, survivors of Colonel Nakaguma's 4th Regiment, supported by eleven medium tanks, would span the Matanikau at its mouth and link up with Oka. The armor had already been brought to the front and was deployed for action.

As Oka and Nakagama squeezed the Americans on the Matanikau, General Maruyama would finish taking Henderson Field in a maneuver he considered his master stroke. The best troops had been selected for it: the 16th and 29th Regiments of the Sendai Division; elements of the 230th Regiment, 38th Division, dismounted cavalrymen, and a battery of pack artillery.

Maruyama had ordered this force to assemble at a stream near Kokumbona. From there, starting October 18, the troops would make a two-day-long forced march through the jungle until they reached the hills just south of Henderson Field.

Maruyama's engineers had been in the jungle several days hacking out a trail for the infantry and artillery. The men of the Sendai Division were already calling it the Maruyama Road. Air reconnaissance had shown the terrain to be rugged, but passable, and Maruyama anticipated no difficulties on the march. His men were tough. Once the 29th Regiment had hiked 122 miles in three days and finished up by double-timing the last mile to show the High Command it could be done.

Hyakutate liked the battle plan. He looked up and beamed, lamplight glinting off the round, silver-framed glasses which gave him an owlish expression. Only one more point needed his consent. That was to approve the place which Maruyama had chosen as the point where the Americans were to surrender. Hyakutate called it a "splendid choice." Beaming, Maruyama saluted, bowed, and strode out to join his troops in their assembly area. The men greeted him with a rousing *"Banzai!"*

"The annihilation of the Americans is about to commence," an officer wrote in his diary. "I thank Heaven for granting me permission to participate in such a magnificent cause. I can barely await the hour of battle . . ."

3

While the Japanese generals were checking their plan of conquest, Admiral Chester Nimitz relieved Admiral Ghormley as Comsopac. His reasons for this were never fully revealed. Ghormley, a quiet, bookish man, had done everything possible to hold Guadalcanal. His superiors apparently wanted a more dynamic man in his stead.

On October 18, as Maruyama's troops started marching to Henderson Field, Nimitz appointed a battle-hardened Pacific veteran, Admiral William Frederick Halsey, to the post of Comsopac. The new commander was known in the Navy as "Bull" Halsey. Sailors on the fighting ships and Marines in foxholes cheered when they learned Halsey was to lead them.

"Old Bull won't take any prize for good looks," a Marine said with a grin, "but he's all fighter and he hates the Japs. I feel a little sorry for Tojo. I wouldn't want Bull Halsey at my throat."

Halsey quickly gave his forces a ringing slogan: *"Kill Japs! Kill Japs! Kill more Japs!"* (This bloodthirsty exhortation was painted in letters three feet high over the boat landing at Tulagi.)

Nimitz did more than merely switch commanders in the South Pacific. He also ordered additional forces into the area. A task force headed by the new battleship *Indiana* was sent through the Panama Canal. The 25th Army Infantry Division moved towards the combat zone from Oahu, Hawaii. Planes, tanks, and artillery were diverted to Halsey. But the United States could not afford to concentrate much strength in the South Pacific.

In October, 1942, America had many global war commitments. The North African landings were being readied. American planes and troops were in England for the invasion of Hitler's Europe, still almost two years away. Ships ferried supplies across the Atlantic where German U-boats sought to carry out the Nazi boast that the "Atlantic shall be a graveyard of ships!"

The U.S. Joint Chiefs of Staff differed about risking too much in the Solomons and the South Pacific; places like Guadalcanal, some argued, were only a sideshow; the real struggle would come in Europe.

Discussion seesawed back and forth until October 24, when President Franklin D. Roosevelt brought it to an end. He ordered reinforcements for Guadalcanal to begin "at once."

As all this toplevel debate was going on in Washington, Marines, and GIs on The Canal could tell the enemy was about to pull something big. Daily patrol clashes grew fiercer along the Matanikau and the Japanese showed more spirit than they had in weeks. The Americans remained alert to an attack from any direction at any time.

Actually, General Maruyama's well-planned offensive had run into trouble. On October 20, he radioed back to

General Hyakutate at Kokumbona that his troops were not yet in position behind Henderson Field. The Maruyama Road presented unexpected difficulties. Ravines, razor-back hills, and bogs not revealed in aerial photographs were blocking the way. The engineers were doing their best, but progress was slow.

Could not the attack be delayed until October 26, Maruyama requested. He promised to have his men in place by then.

To show he had not lost confidence in the success of the operation, Maruyama asked whether he had remembered to remind General Hyakutate that when Vandegrift arrived at the surrender point, he must be alone, except for an interpreter?

Hyakutate was not put off by this attempt to placate him. "General Maruyama is drinking his victory *sake* before the cup is filled," he purportedly grumbled to an aide.

Perhaps Hyakutate would have delayed the Matanikau attacks until Maruyama was ready had he not been under pressure from the Navy. Admirals Kondo and Nagumo bombarded him with a host of peevish messages.

Did the general have to be reminded, they asked, that the Combined Fleet could not remain at sea indefinitely, steaming back and forth while the Army fumbled about? Perhaps the Army lacked courage to attack the Americans?

Hyakutate raged at this impudence. What did sea-going idiots know about the problems of a land campaign? Afraid!

He'd show Kondo and Nagumo! Signaling the fleet that he was attacking, Hyakutate ordered his artillery into action against Blue Battalion, 1st Marines, posted along the ridges that dominated the Matanikau's mouth.

All afternoon on October 21, the battery of "Pistol Petes" slammed at the Marines. But Vandegrift had reinforced his troops with 105-mm howitzers. The American guns knocked out two "Pistol Petes" and forced the others to change position.

That night (October 21) Colonel Nakaguma sent several companies of his 4th Regiment across the river mouth with the eleven tanks leading the way. When Marine artillery fire disabled one tank, the rest swung abruptly around and disappeared back into the jungle, followed by Nakaguma's men.

Lt. Col. W. N. McKelvy, Jr., Blue Battalion's CO, reported to Vandegrift that he had repulsed a Japanese raid. Later, he reconsidered this estimate of the enemy's effort. The Japanese had never before used so much armor on The Canal. The evidence seemed to indicate the foe had launched a full-scale attack, not a raid. However, it was unusual for the Japanese to quit so quickly.

"The Colonel thought they had something more than rice cooking," a Blue Battalion staff officer said. "We felt good about trouncing the Nips, but it had gone too easily for us. We began wondering why they had broken off the fight before it even started."

General Hyakutate could have provided the answer. The reason for the sudden retreat was that Colonel Oka had again failed to carry out his orders to cross the Matanikau and outflank the Marines. Due to a communications breakdown, word of Oka's default did not reach Hyakutate until ten minutes after Nakaguma's tank-led assault had begun.

"Call off the attack!" Hyakutate bellowed when he learned that only Nakaguma was fighting the Americans.

The order was flashed to the front and Nakaguma fell back after suffering needless losses. For a long time that night, the air waves crackled as Hyakutate berated Colonel Oka, who was probably becoming hardened to public upbraidings by his generals . . .

4

General Hyakutate did not merely scold Oka by radio. On Thursday, October 22, his troops along the Matanikau were astounded to see the Commanding General (CG) of the 17th Army at the front. Hyakutate confronted Oka and ordered him to bring his men across the river against the Yankee left flank.

"He who fails us will be shot! Do you understand, Colonel?" Hyakutate shouted.

Oka bowed meekly and returned to his unit. The CG went back to Kokumbona and rechecked the battle plan. It was sound from every angle. With luck it could be concluded on Friday, October 23. Oka would be across the Matanikau by then, Maruyama would be in a position to overwhelm Henderson Field, and Nakaguma's tanks would break through. It was a cheerful prospect.

But Hyakutate's optimism was only wishful thinking.

Since October 20, he had not even been in contact with General Maruyama, who was engulfed in jungle so dense that it blacked out radio transmission. A man more prudent or less ambitious than Hyakutate might have hesitated to mount a full-scale attack without being sure all his forces were properly deployed. But visions of glory beckoned and the general decided the offensive must start on the night of October 23.

But at H-Hour, 2000 (8:00 P.M.) of the appointed day, General Maruyama was still enmeshed in the jungle and Oka had made only tentative advances to the opposite shore of the Matanikau. Colonel Nakaguma once again hurled an unsupported attack against the Marines. Nakaguma was a man of too much courage and too little discretion. It would have been better had he not been so lionhearted.

He led his men into a blizzard of American artillery and small arms fire. The Marine gunners were so accurate that nine tanks were knocked out in a few minutes. As the last vehicle clanked into the American lines, a Marine, Private Joe Champagne, tossed a hand grenade into the vehicle's treads. The blast threw the tank out of control, and sent it running in aimless circles.

A U.S. self-propelled 75-mm cannon rolled onto the sandbar and fired at the crippled tank. A shell pierced the vehicle's armor, to enter the ammunition locker, and the tank blew up, scattering its fragments over a distance of 200 yards.

Nakaguma's soldiers fared no better than had the tanks. On they pounded in a *banzai* charge. Many were cut down by machine gun fire. Still they pressed forward shouting *"Banzai! Banzai!"* and dying for the Mikado.

Colonel Nakaguma stood in the shallow water, flourishing his sword and crying, "On to victory or death!" That night there was only death for his men. The 4th Regiment met *zemmetsu* or total annihilation. By 2200 (10:00 P.M.) the fighting ended.

At daybreak, Saturday, October 24, even battle-toughened Marines blanched at the slaughter of the previous night. Nothing lived on the sandbar; Japanese bodies were heaped amid the burned out hulks of tanks; the jagged stumps of coconut trees jutted out of the crimson-stained sand like splintered limbs. And the only movement was that of dead Japanese bobbing in the muddy river.

5

Colonel Akinosuke Oka must have spent some time preparing an excuse for General Hyakutate on October 24, the day after the Marines destroyed the 4th Regiment. His report stated: "I sought to accomplish the objective of outflanking the enemy, but they seemed to be planning a firm defense of the region . . . and I held back to regroup my forces . . ."

Both Oka and Hyakutate knew the Americans had no defenses in the sector where the crossing was to have been made. The CG contacted Oka by radio. "You will cross the river at once! Any further delay will be regarded as treason!" Hyakutate said.

Obviously Colonel Oka was reluctant to close with the Americans, but he did not relish a court-martial for treason. That led only to a firing squad. If he must die, then let it be in battle. At last he crossed the river in force, but too close to the American left flank. Outposts of Blue Battalion, 7th Marines, holding the left of the line, spotted Oka's troops moving along a ridge.

"The Japs pulled a boner. With the whole jungle to move in, they popped up right under our noses," a Marine officer gloated.

General Vandegrift reacted quickly to the news that his left was threatened. White Battalion, 7th Marines (Lt. Col. Herman Hanneken) marching to relieve Blue Battalion, 1st Marines, which had wiped out Nakaguma, was shifted to the south and by sunset had dug in on a high ridge to extend the American left flank.

At dusk, October 24, General Maruyama's men, worn by their long and arduous march, finally reached the hills south of Henderson Field toward which they had been toiling for almost a week.

They were now poised to swoop upon the Marines guarding Henderson Field only a few miles away. Having reached high ground, Maruyama was again in radio contact with General Hyakutate. He learned that a naval liaison officer was standing by in Kokumbona to signal the Combined Fleet when word came that Henderson Field had been captured.

Maruyama swelled with importance. He had the most important mission of the offensive. It would sit well with the Imperial Staff when he took the Yankee airfield the next day.

His men reflected their CO's confidence. "By tomorrow our flag shall fly over the airfield . . . Oh, what a divine hour now approaches . . ." a young soldier wrote.

Maruyama went out to inspect his lines. In the van, the 29th Regiment was drawing closer to the Marines at a sector held by Red Battalion, 7th Marines, whose CO, Lt. Col. Chesty Puller, was still unaware of the enemy's presence. He found out soon enough.

A Marine patrolling beyond the perimeter noticed a Japanese officer silhouetted on the sky line of a ridge to the south. The Leatherneck blinked, rubbed his eyes, and looked again. The officer was still there, studying the terrain through his binoculars.

The Marine reported to his patrol leader who notified

Division CP where the information aroused a considerable stir. "Japs to the south of Henderson Field! That's trouble! A bellyful of trouble!" exclaimed an Intelligence Officer.

The 164th Infantry hurried to reinforce Puller. The GIs had barely reached the lines when a torrential downpour started. At the height of the rainfall, just after midnight (October 24), General Maruyama ordered the attack to begin.

The Sendai Division responded to his command. Com-

THE STRUGGLE FOR HENDERSON FIELD

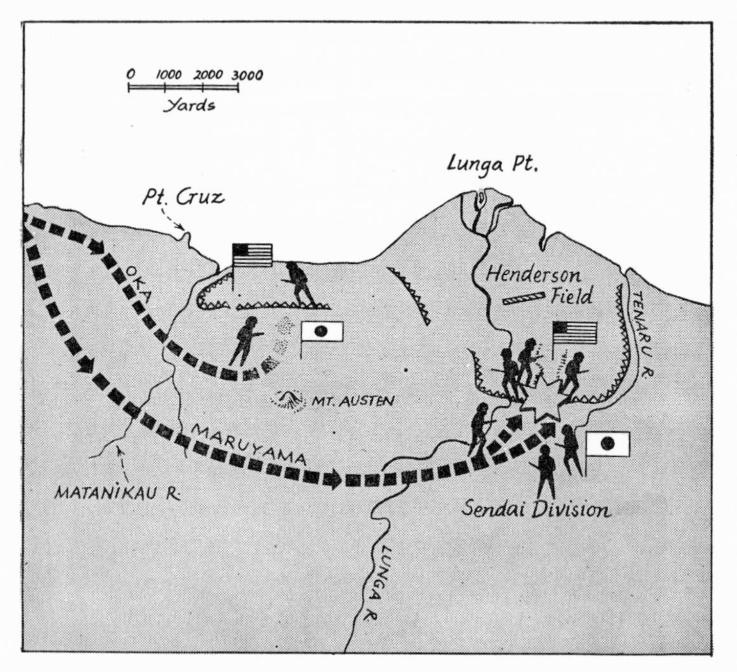

pany after company rushed forward against the Americans. The men slipped in the mud as they charged. When the *banzai*-shouting Japanese reached the barbed wire, U.S. gunners opened up. Sendais fell by the score, but the attack was checked only briefly. The Japanese breached the wire by climbing over it on the bodies of their dead.

The 29th Regiment (Col. Masajiro Furumiya) led the attack at the head of his 7th Company which carried the regimental colors. The color guard was trapped by machine-gun fire between the Marines and the wire. Colonel Furumiya hugged the ground as bullets whipped around him. From time to time, he raised his head and shouted encouragement to the Sendais pressing on in other sectors.

At 0130 (1:30 A.M.) the Japanese were still trying to push the Marines off the ridge. The fighting topped the fury of Bloody Ridge. As the battle raged on, General Maruyama optimistically radioed Hyakutate: "We have prevailed! Long live the Emperor!"

This message was interpreted at Kokumbona to mean that Henderson Field had been taken. The naval liaison officer promptly signaled Admiral Yamamoto: "Airfield occupied! *Banzai!*"

At 0200 (2:00 A.M.) only a half hour later, General Maruyama tempered his earlier despatch by reporting that fighting was continuing. But it was too late by then. Admiral Yamamoto had already ordered the Combined Fleet into action.

6

While the battle for Henderson Field went on, another engagement was taking place about five miles to the west along the left flank of the Marines' Matanikau line. Colonel Oka, still trying to dodge an all-out battle, sought to infiltrate the American defenses.

A group of Oka's men crept up in the rain and massacred a three-man outpost of White Battalion, 7th Marines. The Japanese might have exploited this break in the U.S. line had it not been discovered by Platoon Sergeant Mitchell Paige, whose machine-gun section was dug in on the crest of a hill. Paige heard voices in the jungle below. He listened for a moment and then beckoned the men from their guns. Pointing into the darkness below, he whispered, "Japs!"

The sergeant pulled the pin of a hand grenade and the others followed suit. At Paige's whispered command they hurled the missiles. The jungle muffled the explosions, but not the shrieks that lanced out of the night. The Marines raced back to their guns, expecting an attack. Instead they heard thrashing in the bush, moans, and then silence.

The next morning (October 25) Paige slipped down to scout the base of the hill. He found the bodies of the three-man U.S. outpost and twenty Japanese corpses badly mangled by grenade splinters.

"They must've been bunched up when we dropped the pineapples on them," Paige told his men.

"I guess we won't be having visitors after all," a gunner laughed.

"Don't make any bets on that, Mac," Paige warned. He gestured toward the jungle. "That bush is lousy with Nips and when they come out, we'll have our share of them!"

The sergeant was right. Hanneken's Battalion would have many Japanese "visitors," but not during the daylight hours when the sun made steam rise from the rain-soaked earth. Colonel Oka was waiting for darkness before moving again. As he rested in the jungle the distant booming of naval guns at about 1000 (10:00 A.M.) brought Oka to his feet.

The Imperial Navy was in action. *Banzai!* Perhaps there would be no need for him to attack. It was a hope to which he passionately clung. Oh, let the Navy smash the Americans! Let the Navy do it!

The Navy was certainly trying hard enough. Carriers launched swarms of Vals, Kates, Bettys, and Zekes against Henderson Field. A big cruiser-destroyer force entered the waters behind Florida Island with orders to remain on call. Three large destroyers—the *Akatsuki,* the *Ikazuchi,* and the *Shiratsuyu*—began to bombard the Lunga Point area.

They sank a U.S. Navy tugboat and some small harbor craft when, all at once, the enemy destroyers were bracketed by shellfire from the 105's of the 3rd Marine Defense Battalion. The guns started fires on all three destroyers, which fled at top speed.

Meanwhile the reports reaching General Hyakutate from Maruyama and then passed on to Yamamoto were confusing the admiral. He was not sure who held the airfield.

The latest message admitted that "minor difficulties have been encountered at the airfield . . ." The tone of the despatch convinced Yamamoto that he should not yet commit his main force which continued to circle about 300 miles north of Guadalcanal.

At 1430 (2:30 P.M.) October 25 (a day the Marines would call "Dugout Sunday" because of the constant rain of bombs and shells to which they were subjected) Japanese carrier aircraft reached Lunga Point. The pilots had been told that Maruyama held Henderson Field and anticipated no opposition. Instead, the Japanese fliers ran into a swarm of Wildcats.

Among the Marine pilots was Captain Joe Foss, the top Marine ace. Although on Guadalcanal only 16 days he already had downed a total of eleven bombers and Zeros. On Dugout Sunday, he made four more kills in as many minutes. The Japanese flew off with a loss of 26 planes.

That was not the end of American aerial triumphs for the day. The Imperial Navy's cruisers and destroyers lurking behind Florida Island were ordered out to bombard the American positions. As they came into the open a flight of SBDs caught the ships.

On the first pass, the cruiser *Yura* was hit by a string of 1,000 pound bombs and set afire. Her own destroyers sank the doomed ship with torpedoes at 1700 (5:00 P.M.). The rest of the force raced back into hiding.

Dismay spread among the Imperial Staff. "What is happening? Do we hold the airfield? I demand to know the truth!" Admiral Yamamoto thundered by radio to General Hyakutate.

General Hyakutate had to radio Yamamoto that "due to unforeseen circumstances" the airfield was still in American hands (a fact the Admiral had already deduced after getting a count of his carrier plane losses).

The Army, Hyakutate continued, would try again. "This time with results that will warm our hearts," he assured Yamamoto. His promises did not impress the admiral. Yamamoto sent a sharp message to Hyakutate. The Army had *better* take Henderson Field. A naval battle was shaping up northeast of the Solomons and Yamamoto wanted no trouble from Henderson Field aircraft.

General Hyakutate passed the word along. He sent identical orders to Maruyama and Oka. They stated that: "You *will* attack tonight. Repeat. You *will* attack tonight. Objectives *must* be taken at all costs."

7

The Sendai Division had a motto: "Remember That Death Is Lighter Than a Feather, But Duty is Heavier Than a Mountain . . ."

On October 25, not even the weight of duty equaled the despair crushing the men of the Sendai. All day they sat huddled in the jungle thinking of the comrades lying dead on the ridge slope. The feel of death was everywhere; one saw death in the eyes of the next man; the stench of death hung in the air, intermingled with Guadalcanal's own odors.

This was indeed Death Island. The Sendais shuddered at the memory of what had happened to the 29th Regiment. *Zemmetsu!* Total destruction! Oh, those accursed Marines, those hulking Americans up there on the ridge behind their machine guns. Who could beat such men?

Rumors rustled among the men of the Sendai Division. Colonel Furumiya had been captured and tortured to death by wild Indians the Americans kept for that purpose. Had they heard the Marines were paid a hundred dollars for each prisoner taken? Had they heard . . . The men listened to the fanciful talk and in his heart each was afraid.

Actually, Colonel Furumiya was trapped behind the American lines, but not a prisoner. The color company had met *zemmetsu* beyond the wire. Every man sprawled dead in the trampled mud except for the colonel and an aide.

Furumiya had torn the regimental flag from the staff and wrapped the banner around his waist like a sash. A soldier could suffer no greater disgrace than to let his colors fall into enemy hands. All night the colonel and his faithful officer stumbled about in the jungle seeking a way back to their own lines. They became lost, and with daylight (October 25) hid in a cave to await the Japanese attack that would surely sweep away the Americans as rice husks were blown by wind.

Not only Furumiya and his aide awaited the attack that night. Up on the ridge, Chesty Puller's men also expected it. They were not disappointed. At 2300 (11:00 P.M.) the Marines heard the enemy mobilizing in the jungle. Officers exhorted their men to charge. The Japanese pounded out of the bush chanting, "Yank! Tonight you die!" punctuating that grim prophecy with shrill cries of *"Banzai!"*

But it was the Sendais who died—not the Americans. All night long the enemy went to their deaths under a steady curtain of artillery, 81-mm mortar shells, machine-gun and rifle bullets. Shortly before daybreak (October 26) the remains of the division staggered into the jungle off the ridge that was already known as "Coffin Corner."

General Maruyama stumbled along with his men. He seemed to have aged by many years overnight. No longer arrogant and haughty, he was a beaten man whose eyes were red from weeping over his ruined division. Never again would the Sendais fight as a unit.

Colonel Oka finally attacked over on the Matanikau front with no better luck than Maruyama had. The Battle for Henderson Field ended disastrously for the Japanese. They lost thousands of men without making any gain. Henderson Field had been saved by the blood and courage of the U.S. Marines, soldiers, and airmen. The Japanese had been taught how Americans could fight.

As the beaten Sendai Division tottered westward through the jungle along the same road over which they had so hopefully marched against the Americans, a naval engagement roared up in the placid waters about 300 miles to the east.

Always eager for a surface battle with the U.S. Navy, Admiral Yamamoto sent out his ships with the admonition: "Seek, find, and destroy the enemy! The Emperor is watching you!"

No less anxious for a scrap was Admiral "Bull" Halsey who ordered a task force commanded by Rear Admiral Thomas Kinkaid into the fray with only one order: "Attack!—Repeat—Attack!"

The clash took place on Monday, October 26, off the Santa Cruz Islands, an archipelago lying north of the New Hebrides and to the east of the Solomons. It was a bruising action and both sides took costly losses. The U.S. carrier *Hornet* was sunk by a Japanese sub. In addition, 76 American planes were shot down.

Yamamoto suffered severe damage to two carriers and a heavy cruiser. More than 100 Japanese aircraft were lost to U.S. AA guns and fighter planes. The Battle of the Santa Cruz Islands ended in a draw.

The struggle for Guadalcanal showed no signs of ending. Both sides called up their reserves. General Hyakutate sent back to Rabaul for the last manpower in the 17th Army—his Hiroshima (38th) Division. He had already committed some of Japan's best troops: The Ichiki Detachment, the Kawaguchi Brigade and the Sendai Division. Despite the slaughter of these forces, the Imperial General Staff was still ready to gamble for Guadalcanal. Soon, about 12,000 men of the Hiroshima Division (Lt. General Tadayoshi Sano) would come down the Slot to renew the battle for Death Island.

FURY OFF SANTA CRUZ ISLANDS

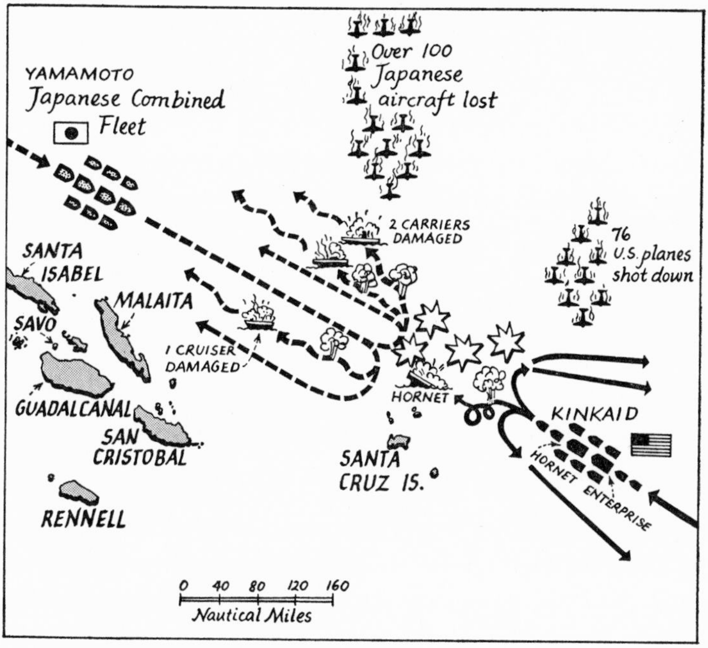

Admiral Halsey also poured more manpower into Guadalcanal: the 132nd Infantry, the 181st Infantry, the 182nd Infantry, plus ships, planes, and equipment.

After the Battle of the Santa Cruz Islands, skirmishes flared up sporadically along the Matanikau front. The Japanese retreating through the jungle lost scores of men on the march. The dead were strewn along the trail. Among the fallen lay Colonel Furumiya and his aide. A Marine patrol found his body near the shreds of his colors. He had shot himself. Nearby sprawled the aide, also a suicide. A note taken from Furumiya's body read:

". . . I do not know what excuses to give . . . I am sorry to have lost so many brave men . . . I am now going to end my life. Long Live the Emperor! Long Live Japan!"

CHAPTER EIGHT

The Final Phase

NOVEMBER 12, 1942—

FEBRUARY 9, 1943

Eight

1

For the Americans on The Canal, November was the month of trial, the time when one's courage and stamina were tested beyond endurance. General Vandegrift's men balanced on the brink of physical and spiritual exhaustion. Many had been in the lines since August and were beginning to crack under the strain.

"Our world consisted of a few muddy yards behind barbed wire," a Guadalcanal veteran recalled. "We were like primitive man who knew nothing except his own little patch of earth; beyond it lay the unknown, a dark place into which we dared not venture."

The Marines had answered every demand of duty; surely no comparable body of Americans had ever before endured so much, so long.

For ninety continuous days the Marines had faced death. During those ninety days, they had not only been locked in combat, but also ravaged by disease: malaria, dysentery, jungle rot, dengue, beriberi. The Marines who had been sturdy, athletic youths only a few months before, now resembled shrunken old men. Each had lost an average of 20 pounds in weight; some as much as 50 pounds.

Worse than the physical discomforts and dangers, a sense of hopelessness oppressed them. They had blocked every enemy thrust but the Japanese always came back and the work of slaughter had to be done again. The Marines had grown sick of the killing, pain, and agony of battle.

They had seen too much horror. Sleep was a breeding place of nightmares in which a man relived again and again the madness of combat. The Marines hated the night—in the darkness they saw the staring eyes, torn bodies, and mangled corpses of slain comrades, and slaughtered foes.

In addition to all this torment, they felt the U.S. government had let them down. Bitterness distorted the realities of the global war. To the men on The Canal no other campaign had any significance. They needed help and it had reached them only in a trickle despite President Roosevelt's orders to reinforce Guadalcanal.

In this mood, the Marines approached November, 1942. The year was waning, but very few Leathernecks expected to live long enough to greet 1943. Malaria was putting men out of action faster than enemy bullets. In October there had been 1,921 cases hospitalized. That total soared to 3,200 during November.

Morale had never been lower and General Vandegrift decided something must be done. "I couldn't let my boys rot in their foxholes while waiting for the enemy to move. They would have become completely demoralized . . ."

The general mounted an offensive against the Japanese west of the Matanikau River line. On November 1, 5,000 Marines crossed the river with orders to break up enemy concentrations.

At the same time, Vandegrift despatched a striking force to the Tenaru River, where, an Intelligence report stated, the enemy intended to land men for another attack on the U.S. eastern flank. According to the report, the Japanese would come ashore near Koli Point about 12 miles east of the Tenaru River. The unit Vandegrift sent there was Hanneken's Battalion. Its orders were terse. "If the Japs land, push them back into the ocean and feed them to the fishes . . ."

Hanneken's men made a forced march across the Tenaru on November 2 and swept on to Koli Point. After crossing the scum-covered Nalimbu River and the Metapona River to the east, they reached high ground which enabled them to make out, through a driving rainstorm, three enemy transports unloading men and artillery. The wetness had rendered Hanneken's radios inoperative and he watched helplessly while the Imperial Army's 230th Regiment established a beachhead.

When his communications were restored, Hanneken

called for reinforcements. Vandegrift helped him by pulling troops out of the Matanikau offensive and rushing them eastward in boats. The 230th Regiment fought the Marines for almost a week until November 10, when the Japanese lines broke. The Americans smashed through to the beachhead, captured tons of supplies, and killed more than 300 Nipponese.

However, most of the 230th escaped into the jungle and fled in a westerly direction, seeking to reach General Hyakutate who was trying to reorganize his broken forces. Vandegrift decided to pursue them and sent a unique volunteer outfit to do the job—Carlson's Raiders—named for their CO, Col. Evans F. Carlson, who had led his 1,500 men on a successful raid against Makin Island in August and had only recently brought them to Guadalcanal.

The motto of Carlson's Raiders was *"Gung Ho!"*, the Chinese phrase for "Work Together." Colonel Carlson had learned it before the war while serving in the Chinese 8th Route Army. His men were trained to live on a sparse diet, to march long distances, and to work in small groups. They were skilled judo fighters and had been carefully selected both for physical strength and emotional stability. Each had unhesitatingly replied "Yes!" when asked, "Do you think you could slit a Jap's throat without flinching?"

The Gung Ho boys entered the jungle on November 11, and cut all lines of communication except for occasional air drops of rations and ammunition. They dogged the retreating Japs for a month. Except for a few stragglers, the 230th Regiment never reached General Hyakutate. Carlson's men killed 400 enemy soldiers while losing only 17 men. On December 11, 1942, the Raiders emerged from the jungle to report the *zemmetsu* of their quarry.

While Carlson was waging this month-long private war, the climactic battle for Guadalcanal had been fought at sea; a three-day-long death struggle known as the Naval Battle of Guadalcanal.

2

The maritime showdown had come about when a U.S. Naval Task Force under Rear Admiral Dan Callaghan escorted transports, commanded by Admiral Richmond Kelly Turner, which were carrying the 182nd U.S. Infantry Regiment to The Canal.

Callaghan's squadron consisted of the flagship cruiser *San Francisco* plus other cruisers: the *Atlanta* (with Rear Admiral Norman Scott aboard), *Portland, Helena,* and *Juneau.* The destroyers *Laffey, Cushing, Sterett, O'Bannion, Aaron Ward, Barton, Monssen,* and *Fletcher* completed the roster of Callaghan's ships.

On November 11, these destroyers and cruisers covered the landing of the 182nd Infantry Regiment at Lunga Point. They were still there November 12, when flights of Japanese bombers arrived to attack the landing area. Forewarned by coastwatchers, who were on the job again, Admiral Turner was ready for the enemy planes.

The destroyers and cruisers gave AA protection. Fighters went up from Henderson Field. Between the ships' guns and the Wildcats, 31 Japanese aircraft were downed in less than 15 minutes with no American losses.

Even as the Americans were exulting over the lopsided victory, word came that an Imperial Navy task force, commanded by Admiral Nobutake Kondo, which included two 32,000-ton battleships, the *Hiei* and the *Kirishima,* was sweeping toward Guadalcanal.

Only Callaghan's five cruisers and eight destroyers stood between the enemy and a crippling bombardment that might render Henderson Field useless.

It was urgent to hold off Kondo. The carrier *Enterprise,* freshly repaired and refitted, was coming from Nouméa and her planes were scheduled to attack the enemy transports hauling the 38th Division down from Rabaul. They would need to operate from Henderson Field. Despite the odds, Turner ordered "Uncle Dan" Callaghan to attack Kondo.

Like modern Davids, the Americans went forth to battle the Japanese Goliaths. Uncle Dan flashed a signal to his ships: "We want the big ones! God bless you all!"

At 0150 (1:50 A.M.) Friday, November 13, the greatest naval engagement of World War II, up to that time, got underway when Callaghan's force met Kondo's in a furious fight. The destroyer *Laffey* made a daring attack on the *Hiei,* slugging gamely until she was set ablaze by the big guns of the Imperial battleship.

The *San Francisco* scored many hits on the *Hiei* but the giant struck the U.S. flagship with a salvo across the bridge, that killed Callaghan and all his staff. The U.S. cruiser *Atlanta,* crippled by gunfire from several enemy ships, drifted into the path of the *San Francisco's* projectiles and an unlucky hit killed Admiral Scott.

Ships circled in confusion as the guns thundered. Japanese fired upon Japanese; Americans on Americans. Gunsmoke obscured the warships' silhouettes making recognition almost impossible. The U.S. destroyer *Barton,* which had been commissioned just five months before, lasted only seven minutes in action.

She fired a salvo, launched four torpedoes, and then blew up when a tin fish from an enemy destroyer blasted her. The U.S. destroyers *Monssen, Cushing* and *Laffey* went down, as did the cruisers *Atlanta* and *Juneau.* When the latter sank she took with her five brothers named Sullivan.

The sacrifices by Callaghan, Scott, and the sailors who died that night were not wasted. The enemy never reached Henderson Field, but turned tail and ran. Every Japanese ship suffered some damage. The destroyer *Yudachi* was sinking; the *Akatsuki* had taken a mortal wound. Most serious for the Imperial Navy, the great *Hiei* had been torn by torpedoes from the U.S. destroyer *Sterett* and her hull was pierced by 85 shells from American guns.

This battle, described by Admiral Ernest King (CNO) as "the fiercest naval engagement in history" saved Henderson Field. Army and Marine fliers went up in the planes spared by Callaghan's bold action, and winged out to take revenge for the men and the ships that had fallen before the enemy.

CALLAGHAN'S ATTACK

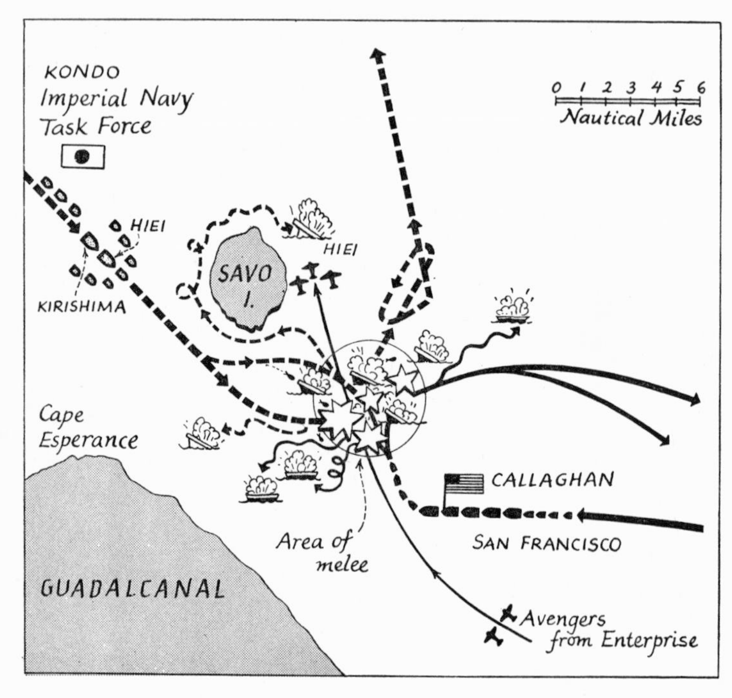

Wildcats shot down eight Zekes flying cover for the battered *Hiei*. An SBD pilot, Major Joe Sailer, wreaked added havoc on the bedeviled giant. He dropped a bomb that demolished the battleship's last AA batteries. The Americans could work without hindrance.

Captain George Dooley led four Avengers in a torpedo attack that shattered the huge ship. More Dauntless dive bombers plastered her with 500 and 1,000 pound bombs. Avengers from the *Enterprise* joined the attack and hit her with torpedoes until the *Hiei* was a mass of glowing white-hot steel. When she finally went under, the battleship left an oil slick that spread over a two mile area of the waters off Savo Island.

3

If nothing else, the Japanese were tenacious. Before dawn on Saturday, November 14, Admiral Gunichi Mikawa came with six cruisers, and six destroyers. He sailed within range of Henderson Field and the heavy cruisers *Suzuya* and *Maya* pumped 1,000 shells onto Henderson Field as Mikawa laid by in his flagship the *Chokai* to cover them.

The two heavies might have caused irreparable damage had not six U.S. torpedo boats (PT) manned by volunteer crews sped from Tulagi Harbor, let fly their tin fish at the enemy ships and raced back to safety. A spread of torpedoes rocked the cruiser *Kinugasa* and caused Admiral Mikawa to lose his nerve. Instead of continuing to pound the airfield, he ordered a withdrawal.

With the enemy gone, a quick survey of Henderson Field revealed damage at a minimum despite the 1,000 shell barrage. Only two planes had been destroyed and 16 needed repairs.

At daybreak (November 14) a flight of Wildcats, SBDs, and TBFs were aloft searching for the retiring bombardment fleet. The Cactus Air Force fliers found Mikawa's ships. They put another torpedo into the *Kinugasa* and planted bombs on two more cruisers and one destroyer.

But there was bigger game for the American pilots that morning. Scout planes reported the approach of eleven transports loaded to the rails with the men of the Hiroshima (38th) Division. The Cactus Air Force men radioed the *Enterprise* to keep her planes after Mikawa's ships while they went off to assault the transports in an operation that became known as the "Buzzard Patrol."

Aboard the Imperial destroyer *Hyashio,* which was escorting the eleven transports through the sun-dappled waters of the Slot, an officer scanned the sky and smiled to himself. No American plane was in sight. Admiral Mikawa's ships, no doubt, had pulverized Henderson Field as he had promised they would. Landing the troops was going to be routine.

The officer glanced at his watch. Noon. They should be

off Tassafaronga in about six hours. He heard airplane motors and looked up to see a line of Dauntless dive bombers streaking down with sunlight dancing on their silvery bodies.

He cried out in alarm as the SBDs hurtled upon the leading transports, ignoring scattered AA fire from sur-

THE DESTRUCTION OF THE JAPANESE TROOP CONVOY

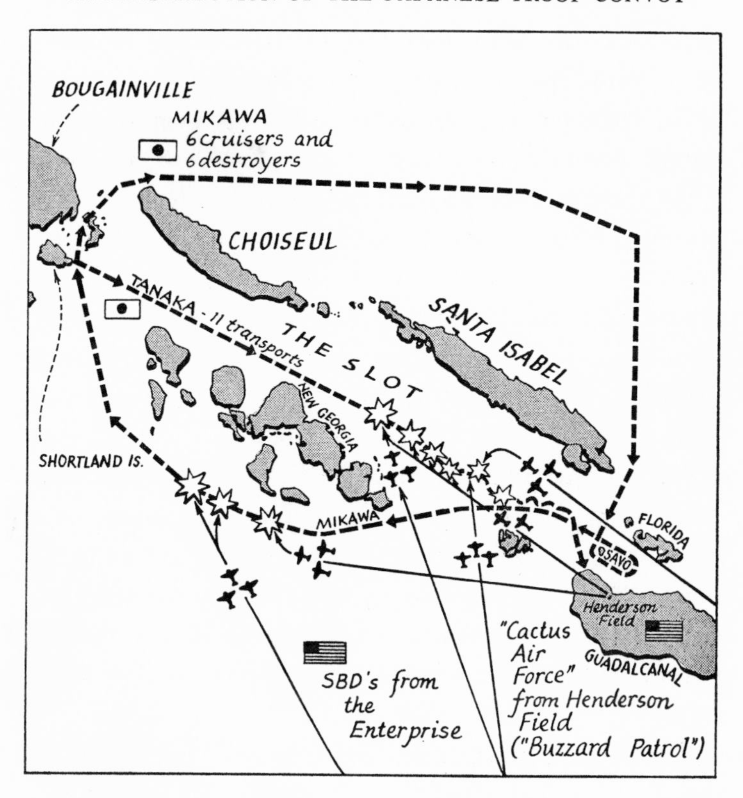

prised destroyers. Thousand-pound bombs tore into the packed steamers with horrifying effect. Sheets of flame shot out of the stricken vessels. The explosions flung men high into the air. The decks of the doomed ships became "a slaughterhouse" according to one American flier.

On and on went the massacre of the Hiroshima Division. Seven transports went down. The four remaining ships, each severely damaged, managed to run aground near Kokumbona where a few hundred soldiers stumbled ashore without leaders or orders.

This group was nearly wiped out by the guns of the destroyer *Meade,* Cactus Air Force planes, and Marine artillery. It had been a day of military and naval disaster never before experienced by the Imperial Navy and the Imperial Army. Only 5,000 men of the 12,000 in the Hiroshima Division survived the carnage.

"The Americans showed no mercy. They are butchers!" a Japanese officer charged.

Admittedly, the American pilots had been merciless for they knew that every Japanese soldier who failed to reach Guadalcanal was one less to deal with later.

"We didn't enjoy our work of slaughter," a Cactus Air Force pilot said. "Looking down at those ships filled with trapped men being pounded to pieces made me sick. But the war made me sick too. Yet by the logic of that day, I could convince myself that the more Japs I killed the sooner the war would be over."

4

Only one more scene remained to be played in that historic naval battle off Guadalcanal. Despite losses and failures, despite the massacre of the Hiroshima Division, Kondo tried to bombard Henderson Field once again, since the original plan of operations had called for shelling the field three nights running. If tenacity was a Japanese virtue, then inflexibility was their greatest flaw.

Just before midnight, November 14, Kondo approached Sealark Channel with the battleship *Kirishima,* the heavy cruisers *Atago* and *Takao,* two light cruisers, and nine destroyers. Confident of success, he believed the Americans had no ships big enough to meet this force.

As far as he knew, no U.S. battleships were in the waters adjacent to Guadalcanal. Even if there had been, he doubted the Americans would risk capital ships in Sealark Channel. According to him, they had neither the audacity nor the skill of the Japanese Navy.

Admiral Kondo was wrong. Bull Halsey had sent Rear Admiral Willis Lee, who looked more like a professor of philosophy than a tough seadog, with the U.S. battleships *South Dakota* and *Washington,* shepherded by four destroyers, on a fast run to Guadalcanal from Nouméa.

As Kondo hove into sight Lee went for him. Another battle was touched off. The Americans quickly lost three of their four destroyers. The *South Dakota* took a beating, but the *Kirishima* was sunk in a broadside duel with the *Washington* of 16-inch guns at point blank range.

The *Atago* and the *Takao* were put out of action for months and the Naval Battle of Guadalcanal concluded in victory for the Americans. The tide had turned. The ordeal was almost over for the 1st Marine Division.

It ended December 9, when the Division was relieved by the U.S. Army. General Vandegrift turned over command of The Canal to General Alexander Patch, CO, Americal

THE NAVAL BATTLE OF GUADALCANAL

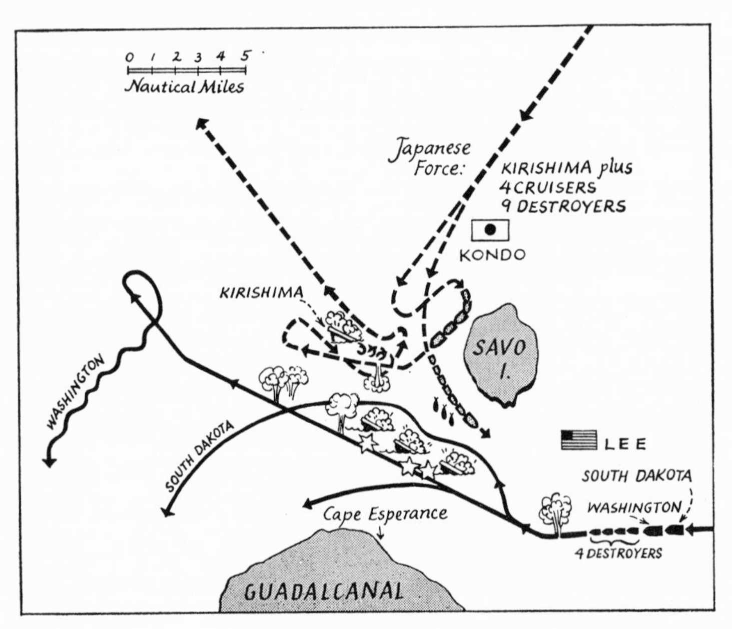

Division. The Marines crept down from the hills after 122 days of unceasing combat; hollow-cheeked, glassy-eyed and gaunt, they stumbled along the trails won by their valor.

They had come to Guadalcanal as boys. Now their youth was spent. Hundreds of them would rest forever on Guadalcanal. Many had suffered wounds. Some had been stricken by illness.

But they were U.S. Marines, always the first to fight. After a long rest, these men would fight again at obscure places with names yet unknown: Tarawa, Saipan, Okinawa, Iwo Jima, New Britain, Betio. Some would fall. Some would be maimed. Some would come home.

The Guadalcanal campaign dragged on another two months. There was more fighting and more dying on land, in the air, and on the sea. But one night the "Tokyo Express" came down the Slot for the last time, to evacuate the survivors of the 17th Army, the men who had believed they were invincible. The rear destroyer of the rescue force took aboard General Harukichi Hyakutate; it was said he wept all the way to Rabaul.

On Thursday, February 9, 1943, a combat patrol of White Battalion, 132nd U.S. Infantry, met a patrol from White Battalion, 161st Infantry, at a village west of the Tenamba River at the westernmost tip of The Canal. They could find no enemy. Only Japanese dead remained.

That day, General Patch radioed Bull Halsey at Nouméa:

"Total and complete defeat of Japanese forces on Guadalcanal effected at 1625 today (4:25 P.M.) . . . 'Tokyo Express' no longer has a terminus on Guadalcanal."

Exactly six months after its beginning, the Guadalcanal campaign ended. In the balance sheet of war the Americans had gained much. The Japanese advance had been stopped. A firm foothold for the long march back to Rabaul and Manila had been hacked out. The human cost in suffering, toil and terror was great, and no statistics could detail the misery endured by the men who had fought on The Canal.

Some 60,000 U.S. Army and Marine Corps troops had been committed there. Of these, 1,592 were killed, almost 4,000 wounded and 7,000 stricken by malaria or other diseases.

Navy losses were never fully compiled, but the toll of dead and wounded probably equalled that suffered by the land forces. Twenty-four U.S. naval vessels, ranging from aircraft carriers to destroyers, were sunk by the enemy. Nearly 100 U.S. fliers gave their lives during the six-month-long struggle.

Japanese casualties were tremendous. The enemy put upwards of 36,000 troops on Guadalcanal. At the end less than 10,000 were evacuated. All the rest died on the island or were taken prisoner. Over thirty thousand lives had been thrown away in a futile struggle to hold an outpost of the Mikado's Empire. No one knows how many thousands more perished aboard blasted transports or barges; nor was any tally kept of the Japanese sailors who went down with their ships. The Imperial Navy also lost twenty-four ships of all types, from battleships to submarines.

Guadalcanal had been a battle of endurance. It forever destroyed the Japanese claims to invincibility and showed the world that free men could fight to win under any conditions.

Guadalcanal's jungles lay silent except for the cries of the birds. Corpses rotted in the bush. The hulks of wrecked tanks rusted in the sun and rain. The tides of war moved by and the deeds done on Guadalcanal grew dim. But long after the fighting had ended, a living ghost brought it back to mind.

On October 27, 1947, a Japanese soldier dressed in a ragged uniform, his hair grown to his waist, emerged from a Guadalcanal cave. This strange creature entered a Solomon Island constabulary post and surrendered. He inquired about the war, for he did not know it was over. Then, in a voice cracked from disuse, he asked, "Where are the American Marines?"

When told they had departed five years before, he sighed and said, "It was no disgrace to be beaten by such men."

BRIEF GLOSSARY OF MILITARY TERMS

AA	Anti-aircraft cannon
AAF	United States Army Air Force
Bushido	Japanese code of military conduct
CG	Commanding General
Cincpac	Commander in Chief, United States Pacific Fleet
Cincpoa	Commander in Chief, Pacific Oceans Area
C.N.O.	Chief of Naval Operations
Comsopac	Commander South Pacific Force and Area
CO	Commanding Officer
CP	Command Post
CTF	Commander Task Force
CTG	Commander Task Group
H.M.A.S.	His Majesty's Australian Ship
H.M.N.Z.S.	His Majesty's New Zealand Ship
LCT	Landing craft tank
O.N.I.	Office of Naval Intelligence
PT	Motor torpedo boat
R.A.A.F.	Royal Australian Air Force
R.A.N.	Royal Australian Navy
RN	Royal Navy
USA	United States Army
USMC	United States Marine Corps

NUMBER OF SHIPS AND TONNAGE SUNK DURING GUADALCANAL CAMPAIGN

	Allied		*Japanese*	
	number	tonnage	number	tonnage
Battleships	0		2	62,000
Aircraft Carriers	2	34,500	0	
Light Carriers	0		1	8,500
Heavy Cruisers	6	56,925	3	26,400
Light Cruisers	2	12,000	1	5,700
Destroyers	14	22,815	11	20,930
Submarines	0		6	11,309
Total	24	126,240	24	134,839

Source: Morison, Samuel Eliot, *The Struggle for Guadalcanal*, Little, Brown and Company, Boston, 1962.

TYPES OF AIRCRAFT IN USE DURING THE BATTLE OF GUADALCANAL

United States

B-17	Flying Fortress, Army, 4 motors, heavy bomber
B-26	Marauder, Army, 2 motors, medium bomber
F4F	Wildcat, Navy, 1 motor, fighter
P-38	Lightning, Army, 2 motors, fighter
PBY	Catalina, Navy, 2 motors, patrol seaplane
SBD	Dauntless, Navy, 1 motor, dive bomber
TBD	Devastator, Navy, 1 motor, torpedo-bomber
TBF	Avenger, Navy, 1 motor, torpedo-bomber

Japanese

"Betty"	Mitsubishi Zero, 1-2 motors, medium bomber
"Emily"	Kawanishi Zero, 2-4 motors, flying boat bomber
"Kate"	Nakajima 97-2, 1 motor, high level or torpedo-bomber
"Mavis"	Kawanishi 97, 4 motors, flying boat patrol bomber
"Val"	Aichi 99-1, 1 motor, dive-bomber
"Zeke"	Zero-3, 1 motor, fighter

SUGGESTED FURTHER READING

In my research for this book, I consulted official histories, diaries, journals, memoirs, newspapers, magazines, and other periodicals. Anyone interested in reading more about Guadalcanal or the Pacific War in general might profit from perusing some of the titles listed

Blankfort, Michael *The Big Yankee: A Biography of Evans Carlson.* Boston: Little, Brown and Co., 1947.

Boyington, Col. Gregory *Baa Baa Black Sheep: An Autobiography.* New York: G. P. Putnam's Sons, 1958.

Dechant, Capt. John A. *Devilbirds: The Story of United States Marine Corps Aviation in World War II.* New York: Harper & Bros., 1947.

Hayashi, Saburo *Kōgun: The Japanese Army in the Pacific War.* Quantico, Va.: The Marine Corps Association, 1959.

McMillan, George *The Old Breed: A History of the First Marine Division in World War Two.* Washington: Infantry Journal Press, 1946.

Miller, John, Jr. *Guadalcanal: The First Offensive.* Washington: Government Printing Office, 1949.

Morison, Samuel Eliot *The Struggle for Guadalcanal (History of United States Naval Operations in World War II, Vol. V)* Boston: Little, Brown and Co., 1949.

Pratt, Fletcher *The Marines' War.* New York: Wm. Sloane Associates, Inc., 1948.

Tregaskis, Richard *Guadalcanal Diary.* New York: Random House, 1943.

Zimmerman, Maj. John L. *The Guadalcanal Campaign.* Washington: Government Printing Office, 1949.

INDEX

IRVING WERSTEIN

Irving Werstein has made writing both his goal and his life. Even when he was officially a factory worker, a salesman, or an actor, Mr. Werstein spent his free moments writing. After serving in the U.S. Army from 1941–45 he devoted all his time to his writing. He has written magazine stories, television and radio scripts, and a number of books.

He was born in Brooklyn, New York, and has lived in Mexico, Italy, and England; he has traveled to Holland and Denmark. Mr. Werstein, his wife, and his son now live in Stuyvesant Town in lower Manhattan.